BRIGHT NOTES

THE IMPORTANCE OF BEING EARNEST AND OTHER WORKS BY OSCAR WILDE

Intelligent Education

Nashville, Tennessee

BRIGHT NOTES: The Importance of Being Earnest and Other Works
www.BrightNotes.com

No part of this publication may be used or reproduced in any manner whatsoever without written permission, except in the case of brief quotations in critical articles and reviews. For permissions, contact Influence Publishers http://www.influencepublishers.com.

ISBN: 978-1-645424-52-9 (Paperback)
ISBN: 978-1-645424-53-6 (eBook)

Published in accordance with the U.S. Copyright Office Orphan Works and Mass Digitization report of the register of copyrights, June 2015.

Originally published by Monarch Press.
Grace Horowitz Schwartz, 1966
2020 Edition published by Influence Publishers.

Interior design by Lapiz Digital Services. Cover Design by Thinkpen Designs.

Printed in the United States of America.

Library of Congress Cataloging-in-Publication Data forthcoming.
Names: Intelligent Education
Title: BRIGHT NOTES: The Importance of Being Earnest and Other Works
Subject: STU004000 STUDY AIDS / Book Notes

CONTENTS

1) Introduction to Oscar Wilde — 1

2) Introduction to Queen Victoria's England — 11

3) Introduction to The Plays — 24

4) Lady Windermere's Fan — 34

5) A Woman of No Importance — 54

6) An Ideal Husband — 73

7) The Importance of Being Earnest — 93

8) Critical Commentary — 123

9) Essay Questions and Answers — 130

10) Bibliography — 142

11) Suggestions for Further Reading — 146

INTRODUCTION TO OSCAR WILDE

EARLY LIFE

Oscar Wilde was born in Dublin, Ireland, on October 16, 1854. At his christening, he was burdened with the lengthy name of Oscar Fingal O'Flahertie Wills Wilde. His parents were both distinguished, though a little peculiar.

His father, Sir William Wilde, was an eye and ear surgeon of world-wide fame. He wrote a textbook on the surgery of the ear that was one of the authorities in its field. Medical students came from all over to study with him. Among his many other interests were medical statistics, literature, and ancient civilizations.

Physically, Sir William Wilde was not very impressive; he was small, homely, and none too careful about cleanliness. All the same, he was constantly involved in love affairs, until one of them turned into a great scandal and injured his career.

Wilde's mother, Jane Elgee, was a bookish woman; under the pen name "Speranza" she wrote many fiery articles in favor of Irish independence from England.

In their Dublin mansion, the famous doctor and his stately literary wife gave many parties and receptions, entertaining most of the famous people of their day. The conversation at these parties was stimulating and the household offered warm hospitality. Mrs. Wilde was apparently more interested in Irish independence than in housekeeping, however. Many stories have been told of her eccentric behavior. It is reported that she once scolded a servant for putting the plates in the coal scuttle; she ordered them to be put on a chair, where they belonged.

Wilde's mother was devoted to him, though she had originally regretted that he was not a girl (she even dressed him in girl's clothing). She stood by him in the difficult years of his later life.

As a boy, Oscar was sent first to Portora Royal School and then to Trinity College in Dublin. At both, he was unpopular because he absolutely loathed sports. However, he was large and powerful though clumsy; when it was necessary, he could more than hold his own in a fight. Oscar was a lazy student. He would not make any effort to learn subjects that did not interest him, such as mathematics and science. But he loved Greek literature. Since he had a powerful memory, he was able to remember what he read. And as he already was showing writing ability, he was able to write with skill in the Greek language. His performance in classical studies was good enough to win him scholarships, as well as a gold medal. In 1876, he entered Magdalen College of Oxford University.

Teaching at Oxford were the great writers John Ruskin and Walter Pater (see previous section). Wilde was impressed by Ruskin's great sincerity as he preached about the horrors of factories and the beauty of honest labor. He was even more impressed by Pater's elegant, musical prose and daring ideas. The thought of tasting life fully, of filling each moment with an experience of the senses, dazzled him. He was not troubled by the fact that this philosophy had no place for moral responsibility or service to one's fellow men. Pater's essays on the Renaissance inspired Wilde, but he never liked Pater himself. Nor did Pater, who was shy and somewhat cold, care for his eccentric student.

Wilde retained his hatred of sports at Oxford, but he was popular because of his good nature, his excellent parties, and his growing conversational ability. He could speak easily on any subject; his conversation was gay, sometimes preposterous, sometimes beautiful, but always entertaining.

Already, he showed a tendency to behave artificially in order to be the center of attention. It is said that once he pointed to a blue china vase in his room and said: "Would that I could live up to my blue china!" This remark had in it a germ of sincerity; it demonstrated Wilde's growing conviction that the beauty of a physical object was a positive good in itself; this was part of the aesthetic creed. (See previous section.) But there is no doubt that he was purposely exaggerating; he was genuinely surprised to learn that some people were foolish enough to take him seriously.

During this Oxford period, Wilde took several important trips abroad. In 1875 and again in 1876 he went to Rome. There he was so moved by the majestic beauty of the Vatican and by an audience with the Pope, that he considered becoming a Catholic. He did not do so, however.

With an old professor of his from Trinity College, J. P. Mahaffy, Wilde visited Greece in 1877. To see the things he had studied and dreamed about for so long was an intoxicating experience. The beauty of Greece influenced him for the rest of his life.

Again at Oxford, Wilde did splendidly in his classical studies. He added another triumph to his academic career when he won the famous Newdigate Prize for poetry with his poem "Ravenna." At the end of his university career he had a great reputation, but no definite plans for his future.

LONDON AND AMERICA

After Oxford, Wilde came to London in 1880. There he set out to make himself well known as quickly as possible. He took the pose of a highly aesthetic young man who devoted himself entirely to beautiful costumes. In the daytime he dressed like a fashionable dandy. But in the evening he blossomed in a costume of his own invention, which consisted of knee breeches, black silk stockings, a velvet coat, a silk shirt, and a large bow tie. In his buttonhole he wore a lily or a sunflower.

Because he was the friend of many aristocratic Oxford graduates, Oscar was made welcome by the great families of London. His eccentric pose, added to the real wit of his conversation, made him a colorful visitor. Soon his exploits and his amusing remarks were the talk of London. It was reported that he claimed to have sat up all night to care for a sick primrose. One story was that he had arrived at a certain house, gorgeously dressed, at dinner time, and said to the owner: "I have come to dine. I thought you would like to have me." Not only had he not been invited, but the man had never set eyes on him before.

Soon the comic magazine *Punch* took up Wilde as a subject. He was caricatured with his knee breeches and his lilies. His eccentricities were reported and exaggerated, and when *Punch* ran out of real life absurdities, it invented more.

More important than this was his contact with Gilbert and Sullivan. In 1875, William S. Gilbert, the lyricist, and Arthur Sullivan, the composer, had begun to collaborate on comic operas. They had several successes, including *Trial by Jury, H.M.S. Pinafore,* and *The Pirates of Penzance.* Now Gilbert was looking around for a new subject, and he got the idea of writing a comic **satire** of the modern aesthetic poets. In 1881, *Patience,* or *Bunthorne's Bride,* was ready. Bunthorne, the leading character, combined the most conspicuous traits Gilbert could find among the new poets. Probably he was meant to be more like Swinburne (see previous section) than anyone else. Bunthorne was known as "the fleshly poet," which describes some of Swinburne's poetry accurately. Also Gilbert's drawings of Bunthorne (which can be found in most of Gilbert's librettos) show a tiny man with a skinny neck and a great mop of hair. The resemblance to Swinburne, who was so little that he was almost a dwarf, and who had a conspicuous head of red hair, is marked. But the love of lilies and the aesthetic talk are taken from Wilde. Tactfully, the resemblance to Wilde was stressed in the production, for by then Swinburne was living under the care of his friend, ruined by his unbalanced excesses, and to make fun of him publicly would have been unthinkable.

Rupert D'Oyly Carte, the producer of *Patience,* wanted to be certain American audiences would understand the joke, so he formed the plan of sending Wilde to America to lecture on aesthetic ideas. It was surely a cruel thing to do, for Carte obviously hoped Wilde would be a laughing stock and thus insure the success of *Patience.*

Most likely, Wilde understood what Carte had in mind. But he had little money and could not sustain his life of elegant aesthetic idleness. He had published a book of poems in 1881, but it had not made much money. Carte's offer was good, so Wilde accepted it in 1882.

In America, Wilde was a sensation. People were surprised at first that he did not wear his funny costumes in the street, and they were disappointed when they found that his lectures were not meant as jokes. But from the moment he left the ocean liner he delighted them each time he spoke. "Have you anything to declare?" the customs inspector asked. "I have nothing to declare except my genius," Wilde replied. Reporters followed him everywhere and eagerly took down everything he said. Ladies appeared in strangely draped costumes which they fondly hoped were aesthetic. And Wilde was swept into a never-ending cycle of balls, dinners, teas, and receptions.

The lectures were well attended. Americans found that Wilde, when he was not making highly affected remarks about flowers and wallpaper, was a most likeable man. He also had the fortunate ability to turn jokes on the jokers. For example, when he lectured at Boston, sixty Harvard students dressed in knee breeches and carrying lilies and sunflowers marched into the lecture hall and sat in the front rows. Wilde somehow found out about the joke ahead of time. He came out on the stage wearing beautiful evening clothes, a picture of conservative elegance in his black suit and white dress shirt. The Harvard men sat foolishly before him, as Wilde skillfully captured the sympathy of the audience.

Several attempts were made to embarrass Wilde by giving him too much to drink, but at Oxford he had developed the ability to out-drink almost anybody. He was able to drink and eat until his hosts lay helpless under the table, a talent which earned him respect from miners and cattlemen when he toured the west.

Altogether, Wilde delivered over eighty lectures. He returned home successful and with a substantial sum of money.

THE CREATIVE YEARS

In 1884, he married. His bride was Constance Lloyd, a very pretty girl with whom he was deeply in love. She in turn was devoted to him. His wife had a moderate income of her own, but the Wildes lived in an elaborate manner, and money continued to be a problem. The profits of the American tour had been spent long before. Wilde tried various ways of earning more. From 1887 to 1889 he was the editor of a woman's magazine. Between 1885 and 1890 he had the less unlikely task of reviewing books for the *Pall Mall Gazette*. He published short stories, essays, and poems in various magazines. A collection of beautiful fairy tales, *The Happy Prince and Other Tales*, appeared in 1888. A collection of short stories and another book of fairy tales followed.

The Picture of Dorian Gray (1891) was Wilde's only novel. It was the story of a beautiful young man who remains untouched by his life of sin, while his portrait exhibits the ravaging of his soul. The morbid atmosphere which fills the book was a terrible shock to the critics, who condemned it violently.

Two melodramas by Oscar Wilde had been produced in New York - *Vera* and *The Duchess of Padua*. They had little success; today's readers do not find this surprising, since both plays are little better than third rate. But their author understood that a really popular play might earn a lot of money. He went to work seriously and within a few weeks had turned out *Lady Windermere's Fan* (1892).

Both critics and public were delighted by this play. Wilde wrote two more plays that followed the same formula as *Lady Windermere's Fan*; these were *A Woman of No Importance* (1893) and *An Ideal Husband* (1895). His method was simply to take a commonplace plot full of melodrama and sentimentality, and decorate it with his own brand of wit, which he usually put into the mouths of a few minor characters. Each of the plays, like most of this writer's work, was dashed off in a spurt of spontaneous creation within a few weeks.

This series of successful plays was ended with *The Importance of Being Earnest* (1895), Wilde's masterpiece and one of the delights of English literature. Within a few short weeks after it opened to the cheers of a fashionable London audience, Wilde's life lay about him in ruins. From 1895 to 1900, the year of his death, his story is one of disaster.

THE DISASTROUS YEARS

One of Oscar Wilde's closest companions was Lord Alfred Douglas. Douglas' father, the Marquis of Queensberry (the same man who invented the Queensberry Rules for boxing), loudly expressed his disapproval of this friendship. At last, Queensberry became publicly insulting; Wilde felt that there was nothing for him to do except to sue Queensberry for libel. He was encouraged by Douglas, who had been on bad terms with his eccentric father since childhood. The fashionable world settled back happily; it expected a particularly juicy scandal at the libel trial, and it was not disappointed.

Wilde's libel suit against Queensberry was suicidal. He was suing Queensberry for soiling his reputation with untrue accusations of homosexual behavior. But in fact these accusations were true; Queensberry's lawyers were able to find evidence and witnesses easily. Wilde took the witness stand to testify. He was then cross-examined by Queensberry's lawyer, Sir Edward Carson. By the end of this extensive cross-examination (which is a classic that is still studied in law schools), it was clear that Wilde was guilty of the charges Queensberry had made. Wilde's lawyers withdrew the suit.

Wilde's friends were sure that he would shortly be arrested; they begged him to flee the country. This he refused to do. Perhaps there is some truth to the explanation that he so loved being the center of attention that he could not bear to flee the spotlight. He was arrested, tried, and sentenced to two years in prison.

The treatment Wilde received from Victorian England fills the twentieth-century reader with dismay. Not only was he imprisoned for what today is regarded as a sick condition, his destruction was received with glee by London society. The very people who had looked up to him, who had enjoyed his stories, jokes, and witty remarks, who had been proud to have him as a guest, now turned on him viciously. His friends deserted him in crowds. While he was free on bail, he was hounded from public places. He could not find any place to sleep at night. There was neither financial aid nor pity for his unhappy wife and little two boys. One actor who had appeared in his plays (and to whom Wilde had never done any harm that we know of) gave a dinner party to celebrate his conviction.

Two years of brutal imprisonment nearly killed Wilde. He was never the same afterward. One of the most pitiful effects was that he could never again sleep uninterruptedly through the night. In prison, he had to undergo inspection every morning, and if a single thing was not in its proper place, he would be harshly punished. He formed the habit of waking several times a night and feeling about him in the dark to make sure that all his possessions were in their proper place. Even after his release, he still did this.

From 1897 to 1900, Wilde lived outside of England, mostly in France, aided by a few faithful friends such as Robert Ross and Robert Sherard. He died, in great agony, of meningitis on November 30, 1900. Two days earlier he had become a convert to the Roman Catholic faith.

Almost entirely drained of creative energy, Wilde was sure he could never write again after he left prison. But he did produce "The **Ballad** of Reading Gaol" (1898), a moving poem about what happened in prison while a condemned man was hanged. It showed a depth and strength which were new in Wilde's work. Prison almost destroyed him, but there seems no doubt that in some ways it also made him grow.

Oscar Wilde's wife and career testify that Victorian England had little room for individuality. With a heavy hand it either forced the uncommon person into conformity or drove him into violent rebellion or unprofitable eccentricity. In a society which was often narrow, ugly, and cruel, Oscar Wilde did not have the wisdom and genius of a William Morris, who could lead a moral crusade against that society's faults. His protest was less powerful, conscious, and direct. It was frittered away in foolishness and weakness. But it was not entirely unproductive.

QUEEN VICTORIA'S ENGLAND

Every writer is marked by the age in which he lives and writes. Oscar Wilde (1854-1900) passed the whole of his short life in the reign of Queen Victoria. In his own unique way, he was as much affected by this fact as was Alfred Lord Tennyson, who is usually thought of as the supremely representative poet of Victoria's world, or Rudyard Kipling, who is known as the spokesman for Victoria's worldwide empire, so farflung that the sun never set on it.

When Victoria became queen in 1837, the royal family was neither popular nor respected. George III, her grandfather, had suffered recurrent spells of insanity during his lengthy reign (1760-1820) and at last, in 1811, he became hopelessly incompetent; the Prince of Wales, the oldest of his ten sons, became Prince Regent. When his father died, he came to the throne as King George IV.

The new king had a history that did not inspire loyal affection. He was married to a Mrs. Fitzherbert in 1785, but the marriage, though blessed with many children, was not recognized officially because the lady was a Roman Catholic instead of a member of the Church of England. George's endless extravagances landed him in hopeless debt. In 1795, he deserted Mrs. Fitzherbert to marry

Princess Caroline of Brunswick on condition that his debts should be paid off.

He made no pretense of caring for the Princess; he first neglected, and then abandoned her. A furor was created when, in 1820, Caroline indicated that she expected to be crowned Queen alongside her husband. George tried to divorce her on the charge that she had committed adultery; the obvious opportunism of his behavior made him thoroughly unpopular. The scandalous situation was climaxed by a scene at the coronation when the Queen tried to enter Westminster Abbey for the ceremony and had the doors shut in her face.

George died without legitimate heirs in 1830. His brother, the Duke of Clarence, succeeded him as William IV. William's outstanding characteristic was his boorishness. His uncouth behavior during his short reign did nothing to win back the respect lost by his father and his brother. It was not expected that young Victoria, who became Queen in 1837, would be able to retrieve the love of the English people which her grandfather and uncles had managed to alienate. In fact, many thinking people assumed that the time of the monarchy was running out. It was expected that Britain would get rid of her royal family, by revolution or by other means, and at last become a republic. It was a strange beginning for what ironically turned out to be the longest reign in English history, more than sixty-three years.

Victoria's father was the Duke of Kent, fourth son of George III. He was the oldest surviving son after King William IV, so that it was understood that his little daughter would eventually become Queen. The Duke died while she was a baby. Her German mother supervised her education with great strictness. This consisted of constant drilling in manners and duties, rather than intellectual training. Thus, though Victoria had considerable intelligence, she did not have the asset of a thorough education. This was to lead, later in life, to a narrow outlook, a serious lack of mental flexibility; even today, we think of this cast of mind as "Victorian."

But in 1837, no misgivings about the Queen's limitations troubled England. The people only knew that after a succession of elderly, unappealing kings, they now had a queen who was eighteen years of age, attractive, vivacious, and conscientious. A great wave of affection rose from her subjects, and with this there was mingled a protective instinct. The Queen was hardly more than a child. She had been chaperoned and protected; diligently, those in charge of her had shielded her innocence from contact with anything distressing or improper. Now her subjects began to shield her too. Statesmen, artists, and writers shared an impulse to avoid those subjects that might be unsuitable for the sheltered young queen.

Thus, the accident that the English crown was inherited by a girl colored the culture of an entire age. The effect was striking - and not entirely desirable. What may be proper intellectual nourishment for a strictly raised eighteen-year-old girl is not necessarily appropriate for all the people in a country. Also, the result was the encouragement of respectability, not the rebirth of virtue. These are quite different things. If, inspired by the Queen, the British people had shown an impulse toward higher standards of conduct, the result would surely have been impressive. But as a whole they did not do this. Rather, they showed a greater interest in appearing respectable. The opinion of one's neighbors became all-important. As a result, hypocrisy became the most important virtue. The standard of conduct in Victoria's time was extremely strict and the penalty for breaking the moral code was to be cast out from society - but this meant in practice only that one was expected to avoid getting caught.

Thus, the Victorian era fostered a highly repressive atmosphere. What one could or could not do was carefully prescribed by society. And with this went an insincerity which came to be accepted as entirely natural, especially by the middle class.

Victoria's later history did nothing to alter this. Married to her German cousin Albert, whom she adored, she became the mother of nine children. In 1861, Albert died suddenly, leaving the Queen an inconsolable widow. For the remaining forty years of her life, she wore mourning for him. Naturally, the domestic virtues were those most prized by the Queen. As she got older she became even surer that her own limited ideas were the only correct ones. As an example, for many years she refused to receive at court any woman who had been widowed and had later remarried. She expected all women to abide by her idea of how a widow should behave. She demanded that all women who hoped to take part in the life of the royal court live according to standards that were in excess of what any western religion required.

To summarize, the atmosphere of Victorian England was stuffy and hypocritical. It insisted on conformity. As a result, it produced a large number of people obedient to its standards- but it also produced a crop of colorful eccentrics and rebels. Oscar Wilde was one of these.

SCIENCE AND RELIGION

In 1859, Charles Darwin published his book, *On the Origin of Species by Means of Natural Selection*, which presented the theory of evolution and touched off a violent controversy which has not subsided completely even today. However, we must not make the mistake of assuming that Darwin was the first person ever to have such ideas. Even in ancient Greece, certain philosophers had suggested that the forms of living things tended to change and develop as time passed. In the early nineteenth century, a French scientist, Baron Cuvier, observed in fossils simple forms of life which had once existed on the earth but were no longer to be found. Sir Charles Lyell explained the enormous extent of geological time in Principles of Geology (1833).

Darwin incorporated a lot of earlier material with his own observations to produce his theory. To put it simply, Darwin observed that most species of plants and animals produced far more young than ever grew into maturity. In the case of some of the simpler organisms, only a minute percentage of those produced could survive. He pointed out that if all the oysters produced in one year were to reach maturity and reproduce, great mountains of oysters would tower up out of the oceans.

What was it that determined which organisms out of the multitudes would be the survivors? Darwin answered that the huge numbers of organisms produced by a given species had a great variety of hereditary characteristics. Those who happened to have characteristics that helped them catch their food and avoid their enemies were the ones that lived. The others died, victims of their enemies, starvation, or other kinds of destruction. Among characteristics that might be helpful to survival were speed, strength, and protective coloration that helped the organism to blend with its surroundings and avoid being seen.

Darwin reasoned further that those creatures that survived were the ones that reproduced themselves; they passed their characteristics on to at least some of their offspring, who then could also survive and reproduce. Those creatures who did not last till maturity died out before they could reproduce themselves. In this way, those characteristics useful in the environment were perpetuated. Thus, the various species developed and changed their characteristics.

Darwin was convinced that this process had been in effect countless millions of years; he believed it had begun with a primitive unicellular sea creature that had been the first life on the earth. As a result of the constant operation of this process, different kinds of life had developed. Some kinds had died out and could now be seen only as fossils. Others became more and more differentiated and complex, until the various forms of plant and animal life known in the modern world came into being.

Naturally, not many people actually read through Darwin's complex and technical explanations. But his ideas became known through newspapers, magazines and sermons. For the implications were clear. If life really had begun in a very simple form and slowly developed over vast stretches of time, then the account of creation in the Bible was seemingly contradicted- for this was different from a world made with all its varied creatures within seven days by the hand of God. A famous Biblical scholar, Bishop Ussher, had, after careful study, dated the year of creation as 4004 B.C. He was even able to supply the very day and hour of the event. Now the concept of geological time made this absurd.

Thus it seemed to many that the very foundations of religious faith were being attacked. Yet, eventually, the various sects were able to assimilate Darwin's ideas. Almost all religious groups have faced the contradictions between science and traditional interpretation of the Bible. Evolution is today taught in many religious seminaries. Darwin himself is buried in Westminster Abbey.

Yet Darwin's thought did give a terrible shock to the time. Before him, most people lived in a cozy, understandable world. Man was the center of this world-of course, for was he not made in God's image? All of creation had been for the purpose of providing a home for him. The universe, the Earth, other living creatures, only mattered because they were necessary to man.

But with the new science, how cold and terrifying the universe became! How frightening it was to think of the earth as an insignificant speck in time and space, where a series of evolutionary accidents had produced the human race.

And worst of all were the methods by which evolution took place. The main instrument of it seemed to be death! Huge quantities of living creatures were produced, apparently with no other function but to die. They were linked with one another in a relationship of repeated cruelty and suffering. A creature might be a destroyer of many species, only to fall a victim at last to others more quick or powerful than itself.

How different is this world governed by waste, accident, and cruelty from that secure one where the benevolent Creator observed each sparrow's fall! Many men who could face the idea that the account of creation in the Bible might not be strictly accurate were stricken to the heart by the senselessness and horror of this picture. Alfred Lord Tennyson, a very typical Victorian writer, speaks of Nature, "red in tooth and claw." "How careful of the type she seems,/ How careless of the single life." Nothing could better sum up the despair of the thoughtful man than these excerpets from Tennyson's "In Memoriam".

To summarize, the conflict between science and religion in the Victorian period produced an atmosphere of despair. Thoughtful men found the new world of science, so huge and indifferent to man, a bleak place to live. Some, like Tennyson, faced the problem and struggled to find some basis for faith and hope.

But others, equally aware of the new atmosphere, fought it by ignoring it. They also were troubled by the lonely new world in which they had to live. But they protected themselves by trying to escape. They tried to find a scale of values which would not be affected by these developments. Such men, no longer able to have confidence in the moral world, turned to the world of beauty. The worship of beauty became an end in itself. Beauty was safe, unaffected by outside events. In beauty one could place one's faith and hope; it was changeless. Among those who turned to the worship of beauty were the poet Algernon Swinburne, the critic Walter Pater, and Oscar Wilde.

THE INDUSTRIAL REVOLUTION

Beginning in the middle of the eighteenth century, the face of England was drastically changed by a huge series of events, which we usually call "The Industrial Revolution." In the early eighteenth century, all Englishmen made their living from the land.

The term "Industrial Revolution" refers to the period in English history, approximately 1750-1850, in which major social and economic changes took place. With the invention of the spinning frame and power loom, England moved from an agricultural and commercial society to a modern industrial society. England became a world textile center. By the mid-1840s over half a million people were employed, 340,000 of them tending power-driven machines in factories.

Economists such as Adam Smith and David Ricardo rejected contemporary doctrines. They developed the thesis that division of labor and free trade would necessarily benefit the bulk of the populace. But these new doctrines inherited the squalor of the past centuries and developed some new difficulties.

In 1764 a machine for spinning thread (known as the "spinning jenny") was invented. A series of other inventions followed rapidly, including the steam locomotive in 1825. It became possible to produce cotton, wool, and iron at far lower cost than ever before. This was done by building power-driven machines and assembling them in factories, where large numbers of workers came together to operate them. Most often, these factories were built in the north of England, near the coal mines which provided the fuel that would make steam to drive the machines. It was because of this that the industrial cities of England were built mainly in the north.

England's cities grew monstrously in the years between 1800 and 1830. Thousands who could no longer live from the land came to the cities, where they had a better chance of survival. An entirely new class of people developed-people who were, dependent on factory employment rather than on the whims of nature. As thousands poured into the urban settlements, tremendous new difficulties had to be overcome.

Not enough wealth had yet been produced to adequately provide for the newcomers. No housing had been planned to accommodate the hordes of workers. At first, they lived in abandoned houses in old sections of the cities. Eventually inexpensive housing was put up, built by the barest minimum of speculative capital. Among other things, sanitary conditions were woefully substandard (in relation to our present-day standards) and this led to a severe epidemic of cholera during the 1830s.

The multitudes had come from abject poverty to conditions barely better. It was a brand-new mode of living, but the system was yet too young to alleviate the horrors. English cities were hideous in a way that we of the twentieth century can scarcely imagine. In huddled groups of tumble-down houses, mobs of people lived, sometimes several families in one room. Filth and horrible smells were everywhere. People were dressed in rags. Children were undernourished and deformed. In the mines, five-year-olds pulled carts of coal for twelve to fourteen hours a day and never saw the sunlight-or the inside of a school.

Some writers tried to make the people of England conscious of the horrors all around them. For example, Elizabeth Barrett wrote "The Cry of the Children," which described the conditions of child labor. But for others, the ugliness of industrial England made physical beauty seem more important than ever before. In reaction to what they saw, they regarded beauty as a supreme good. Oscar Wilde is one example of this. His writings show no trace of what we call "social consciousness." He never indicates any concern for the evils of his time. Slums, child labor, disease, and poverty might not have existed for all the notice Wilde takes of them. Reading his plays, one gets the impression that England is made up entirely of Lords, Ladies, and a few others who do not have titles but are at least independently wealthy.

Nevertheless, in spite of the narrow focus and limited sympathy displayed in his work, one gets a strong impression that Wilde turns to elegance and beauty to some extent because the whole of reality is unacceptable to him. He escapes ugliness and doubt, and while he does so, he enables his audience to escape with him.

THE AESTHETIC MOVEMENT

Reaction against the conformity, hideousness, and doubt of nineteenth-century England came to a spectacular **climax** in the 1890s. This rebellion featured a group of eccentric, self-conscious young men, of whom Oscar Wilde was the most famous. But a stream of rebellion can be traced far back to the 1850s. In 1853, in *The Stones of Venice*, John Ruskin presented the theory that England's lack of beauty was simply a visual sign that English life lacked moral good and inner joy; beauty and goodness were part of each other. Dante Gabriel Rossetti was convinced that the Middle Ages were far superior to nineteenth-century England. He was a gifted painter and a fine poet; in both forms he celebrated the beauty and sincerity of medieval life.

William Morris (1834-1896) carried his dissatisfaction with industrialism and mass production even further. He found factory-made objects ugly and worthless; he felt that the only way for the individual to create beauty was to devote himself to craftsmanship and painstaking handwork. In 1861, he formed a company to produce wallpaper, tiles, draperies, carpets, and furniture by old hand methods. The results showed beauty and artistic integrity. Indeed, by this work, Morris created a small revolution and founded the modern art of interior decoration. Morris was also a fine poet.

In Ruskin, Rossetti, and Morris, we find a deep concern with morality and virtue, as well as with beauty. In different ways, each of these men found a close connection between ugliness and evil, and between virtue and beauty. Their love of beauty was part of their devotion to what was good.

But as time went on, the idea of beauty no longer was firmly connected to the idea of goodness. The poet Algernon Swinburne was a violent hater of all authority, political and religious. He praised the joys of passion and the beauty of the pagan way of life. This brought down the wrath of conventional Victorians on his head; he was condemned for being indecent and irreligious. Poor Swinburne was an unstable person at best, and after years of alcoholism and other excesses, he broke down completely in 1879, at the age of forty-two, while his respectable enemies enjoyed the opportunity to cry: "I told you so!" For the remaining thirty years of his life, he lived under the careful control of his friend, Theodore Watts Dunton. Eventually, he became able to write again though his great work was all done in the 1860s and 1870s.

Many ideas which can be seen in Swinburne's passionate poetry were given formal expression by the influential essayist Walter Pater (1839-1894). As a student at Oxford, he had intended to become a clergyman, but he became skeptical toward religion. He became a fellow at Brasenose College, Oxford, where he influenced students for many years. Pater wrote extensively about the art of Italy and Greece. His essays showed much sympathy with pagan thought. Beauty was his great ideal. He praised "art for art's sake." That is, beauty was not for creating moral goodness; it was sufficient in itself. "The perfect and complete enjoyment of something beautiful was the greatest happiness a man could know," Pater stated. He wrote that to each man only a limited number of moments is given; the best use a man can make of them is to fill each one with an exquisite sensation.

Pater was himself a mild little man; but he was worshiped by Oxford students who abandoned conventional behavior and tried to follow his instructions. They tried to live each moment to the fullest-to "burn with a hard, gemlike flame," as

Pater recommended. Wilde was among the students who were influenced by him.

Thus, the serious moral rebellion against ugly Victorian materialism which we find in the 1850s and 1860s eventually alters until it loses its ethical side completely and becomes a delight in pleasurable sensations. By the 1880s, the "aesthetic movement" was in existence; Wilde was its best known disciple. Others were Arthur Symons and John Addington Symonds. "Aestheticism" may be defined as a philosophy which makes appreciation of beauty through man's senses the chief aim of life. Ridiculing the Victorian **conventions** with his sophisticated wit, Wilde praised the free enjoyment of pleasure as an ideal of life.

He claimed that the pagan Greeks had lived in this way. However, in fact Wilde's ideas were also much influenced by the French literature of his time. Among these influences were Emile Zola, who permitted himself, in his realistic novels, to discuss what had been impossible to mention before. The poet Baudelaire, author of *Flowers of Evil*, also was an important influence; he delighted in evil, which had a weird beauty for him. Also Flaubert, the author of *Madame Bovary*, showed the English aesthetes how one could polish and perfect one's language as though it were sculpture.

To summarize, the aesthetes of the 1880s and 1890s formed a very sophisticated little group, scornful of conventions, proud of their moral daring, and most anxious to develop extraordinary skill in the use of words. They were obviously the result of a long rebellion against Victorian hypocrisy, scientific materialism, and ugly industrialism; however, they were the indirect product of these things.

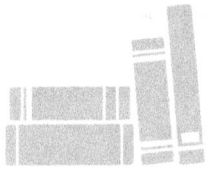

INTRODUCTION TO THE PLAYS

DRAMATIC HERITAGE

English writers have produced some of the greatest plays in the world. In the late sixteenth and early seventeenth centuries, William Shakespeare wrote his plays, which are unmatched in dramatic literature. He was surrounded by other writers who were also great but have been overshadowed by him. In the late seventeenth century, a number of skilled writers wrote highly polished, elegantly artificial comedies. (These are called Restoration comedies, because they appeared during the time King Charles II (1660-1685) was restored to the English throne. Before him, a revolution had turned England into a republic for a number of years.) The English stage was brightened again in the eighteenth century by the comedies of Goldsmith and Sheridan.

But in the nineteenth century, the English theatre came upon bad days. The best writers wrote poetry or novels. Once in a while a fine writer would attempt a play (Robert Browning tried several times), but usually he was unsuccessful.

On the stage, Shakespeare's plays were popular. Only they were so cut, changed around and added to, that probably Shakespeare himself would not have recognized them. These productions were mounted in magnificent style, with spectacular costumes and superb scenic effects. But probably most intelligent people found it more rewarding to stay home and read the play in the original than to attend such performances.

Besides Shakespeare, many modern works were produced. These were usually comedies and melodramas. They were so stereotyped that they tended to resemble one another a great deal, and they were practically devoid of intellectual content- like many routine motion pictures of our own time.

Rescue from this dramatic sterility came in the 1880s and 1890s. Henrik Ibsen, a Norwegian dramatist, and August Strindberg, a Swedish writer, each produced a series of plays, employing brilliant skill, to present highly controversial ideas about marriage, parents and children, and other subjects. These plays translated and produced in England. Bernard Shaw publicized this new style of drama. By 1892, he was beginning to write intelligent, stimulating plays himself.

But even when it came, this new type of play was in the minority for a long time. Most of them were predictable comedies and stereotyped dramas. The Scandinavians, Ibsen and Strindberg, would be the inventors of the revolutionary new drama. The conventional older dramas also had foreign parentage-Eugene Scribe and Victorien Sardou of France.

Eugene Scribe (1791-1861) ruled the French theatre for thirty years, reaching the height of fame in the 1830s. Scribe developed a five-act comic play full of movement and with a twisting, turning plot. He seems to have had a methodical mind, for he developed a system for putting together such comedies. It was so exact that the formula could be easily followed. The story always followed the same outlines. There was an explanation of the opening situation, complications were introduced, the action reached a **climax**, and then everything was straightened out so that everybody who deserved to lived happily ever after. Even the entrances and exits of the different characters were arranged according to a pattern.

With the help of collaborators who wrote under his direction, Scribe ran a sort of play factory that turned out over four hundred works. His collected works run to an incredible total of seventy-six volumes. He stamped his influence on uncounted other plays besides those bearing his name. Wilde's comedies certainly belong to the same family as Scribe's and such comedies still open on Broadway every season.

Scribe believed that the theatre was a place for being amused. He denied that teaching or ideas belonged on the stage.

Victorien Sardou (1831-1908) was of a later generation; he was also influential and popular. His greatest success was in the field of melodrama. (A melodrama is a play full of sad and violent happenings. It does not have characters of great depth, so it does not usually arouse profound emotions on the part of the audience. It sometimes has a happy ending.) Like Scribe, Sardou could put together a play in a neat, efficient manner. His later plays were written for Sarah Bernhardt, the famous actress. Among these were Fedora (1882) and La Tosca (1887). La Tosca later was made into an effective opera by the Italian composer Giacomo Puccini.

WILDE'S DRAMATIC TECHNIQUE

When we turn to the plays of Oscar Wilde, we see that they belong, in terms of technique, to the school of Scribe, Sardou, and innumerable second-rate writers who followed them. It is interesting that *Lady Windermere's Fan* was produced in 1892, the same year as Bernard Shaw's first play, *Widower's Houses*. The two plays came from different worlds. Shaw's play is touched by the spirit of Ibsen and Strindberg. Not a trace of this spirit appears in Wilde's play.

In Wilde's dramas we find the standard ingredients-plot, counterplot, vital secrets, letters which fall into the wrong hands. Wilde handles them very well. It is really surprising that Wilde should have picked up the technique of writing plays so quickly and easily. His plays move well on the stage. A far greater writer, Robert Browning, was unable to put together a playable drama-one that would hold the interest of an audience in a theatre.

But, the plots of these plays show no more than efficient handling. Wilde juggles the standard ingredients in a way Scribe would have approved of. But he does not care about the foolish wives, noble husbands, scheming adventuresses and lost fans. He does not even seem to believe in them. He merely goes through the motions.

These are no personal moral convictions in Wilde's plays. He writes of high society-or at least that is what he calls it, though it does not seem to resemble any real group of people that ever lived. He projects secondhand morality along with secondhand plots. A good woman is the finest influence on a man-if she tempers her strict standards with a little mercy for most of humanity, who are, naturally, not nearly as good as she is. An adulteress is the worst of sinners. However, love conquers all. The love of a mother is the greatest love in the world. And so forth.

Considering that Wilde's plays have little distinction of story or idea, why have they lasted? Why are they still read and acted, when many plays like them have fallen into oblivion?

The answer seems to be that they have one special ingredient-satire. Wilde's blend of criticism, wit, and ironic humor aims at ridiculing the conventional morality of his characters. His cleverness, gaiety, Irish high spirits, and love of the ridiculous - those things that made his personality unique to those who knew him - are transferred to the plays. Usually, he introduces one or two characters who speak as Wilde himself did, or who demonstrate his ability to inject absurdities into the conventional conversations of the characters who are in his plays. For example, in *Lady Windermere's Fan*, Lord Darlington often sounds like Oscar Wilde himself. At one point he remarks: "I can resist everything except temptation."

In the same play, the Duchess of Berwick and her daughter, Lady Agatha, are fine examples of Wilde's gay inventiveness. The Duchess is a nonstop talker who is busy at the serious occupation of getting her daughter engaged to be married. The dutiful Agatha says absolutely nothing in the course of the play except "Yes, Mama." A high point is reached when her mother refers to her lovingly as "my little chatterbox."

Another example of comic inventiveness is the forgetful Lady Markby, in *An Ideal Husband*. She reminisces, for example, about an acquaintance whose life was so unhappy that "she went into a convent, or on to the operatic stage, I forget which."

The above are very minor examples of the wit which decorates *Lady Windermere's Fan, A Woman of No Importance,* and *An Ideal Husband.* Indeed, the finest examples have not been mentioned, in order to give the student the pleasure of discovering them as he reads the plays.

We must add that these generalizations do not apply to *The Importance of Being Earnest.* In this, the last of his plays, Wilde has made certain changes in his methods which are so effective that we may call them an inspiration.

In the earlier plays, Wilde wrote two kinds of material. One was a complex melodramatic play of the sort made popular by Scribe and Sardou. The other was a quantity of witty dialogue, having only a distant relationship to the main part of the play. What Wilde did was to stop the play occasionally and insert a scene of this verbal byplay. It was apparently the same sort of extravagant humor with which he used to entertain his friends. This humor is the best thing by far in the earlier plays, but it does start and stop abruptly. It is not really a part of these plays. That is, most of the best humor in these plays could be removed and still leave the plays practically intact - though dull.

What the author does in *The Importance of Being Earnest* is to make the entire play, plot and characters as well as dialogue, equally ridiculous. Now the verbal humor is integrated with the whole.

For example, the play is about the troubles of two pairs of young lovers-Jack and Gwendolen, and Algernon and Cecily. For a time it seems as though neither couple will be permitted to get married. Jack cannot identify his parents, so that Gwendolen's mother will not consent to their marriage. Algernon and Cecily also meet with disapproval. Then, too, there are temporary misunderstandings between the couples themselves. At one point they quarrel and break their engagements.

This all seems usual enough in outline. However, it begins to take on a unique quality when we add that Jack's parent-substitute is a black leather valise (he was found in it as a baby), and that Gwendolen's mother tells him that this is no basis for a recognized position in good society. She advises Jack to produce at least one parent before the end of the social season. She cannot allow her only daughter to "form an alliance with a parcel."

Also, the basis for the quarrels between the young people themselves is partly that each young lady is determined to marry a young man named Ernest; each is furious when she finds out that her young man is not called Ernest, though he has pretended to be.

The characters have no depth, but they have wonderful vivacity and polish. There is Lady Bracknell, Gwendolen's mother, who is described by her future son-in-law as "a monster, without being a myth, which is rather unfair." Gwendolen is sophisticated and Cecily is naive, but they are both crisply efficient about getting their young men to propose marriage. Dignified Jack and wily Algernon are excellent partners for them.

The minor characters are drawn with equal skill. Miss Prism, the governess, is the very image of propriety - and the only woman in literature absent-minded enough to put a literary manuscript in a baby carriage and a baby in a valise instead of the other way around. Canon Chasuble, the local clergyman, is a superb example of clerical dignity.

Thus we have a complicated plot, full of intrigue, and recognizable characters. But the plot is given the dimension of fantastic absurdity, and the characters are exaggerated until they become caricatures. All this is embodied in dialogue of a kind that is unique with Wilde. The wonderful style is maintained throughout. Even explanations that would be a tiresome necessity in other plays are witty and funny.

STYLE

What are the elements of Wilde's style? A close examination of the plays, especially *Earnest*, will provide the best and most enjoyable answer. But we may attempt to point out a few of its more conspicuous characteristics.

One element is the use of misapplied logic. This is found in dialogue that sounds reasonable but is actually nonsensical. It is similar to the old joke in which a man is asked where the Second National Bank is located and replies that he does not even know where the First National Bank is. For example, Algernon, in Act One, cautions Jack not to eat the cucumber sandwiches, which are for Lady Bracknell. Jack points out that Algernon himself has been eating them steadily. Algernon replies: "That is quite a different matter. She is my aunt." In a later scene, as Lady Bracknell leaves with Gwendolen to catch a train, she remarks: "We have already missed five, if not six, trains. To miss any more might expose us to comment on the platform".

Another element of style is the use of paradox, which is a statement that seems contradictory, unbelievable, or absurd. Lady Bracknell is questioning Jack to find out whether he is a desirable suitor for her daughter. She asks: "You have a town house, I hope? A girl with a simple, unspoiled nature, like Gwendolen, could hardly be expected to reside in the country." (Girls with simple, unspoiled natures are of course usually expected to live in the country.)

In another scene, Gwendolen refers to her father. She says she is glad that nobody outside of his home has ever heard of him: "I think that is quite as it should be. The home seems to me to be the proper sphere for the man." (This turns upside down the common saying that the proper place for a woman is in the home.)

One must also mention the use of the language itself in the play. Line after line is a triumph of glittering, scintillating loquaciousness, so perfect that not a word could be changed without spoiling the effect. Lady Bracknell describes Miss Prism as, "a female of repellent aspect, remotely connected with education." Algernon remarks about a recently widowed acquaintance: "I hear her hair has turned quite gold from grief." Miss Prism describes a novel she once wrote: "The good ended happily, and the bad unhappily. That is what Fiction means."

To summarize, *The Importance of Being Earnest* is a perfect union of plot, character and style. All blend to create something as weightless and luminous as a bubble. That the play is quite frivolous does not make it any less remarkable. Art with a deep purpose is not the only worthwhile kind. Gaiety, polish, elegance - these also have their value.

A NOTE ON SALOME

This strange one-act play has an interesting history. It is the story of Salome, the daughter of Queen Herodias, Princess of

Judea; the other leading character is Saint John the Baptist. The terrible story of how Salome became infatuated with the saint and had him killed by her stepfather, Herod, because he repulsed her, is of course derived from the New Testament.

Wilde converts it into a sinister mood-piece full of weird symbols of blood and death. It is a compelling little study of passion and evil. The language is rich with suggestion. It is quite different from Wilde's usual elegance of expression. The vocabulary is simple; there is much repetition. This gives an understated, almost hypnotic tone to the play.

The style is apparently influenced by that of the Belgian writer, Maurice Maeterlinck. In fact, Wilde wrote it first in French (in 1891) for the actress Sarah Bernhardt. She was hesitant about appearing in it, at the time. The play was translated into English in 1894. It has had a long and successful career, especially in an operatic adaptation (1905) by the German composer Richard Strauss.

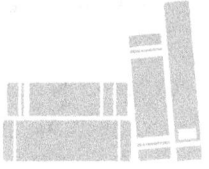

LADY WINDERMERE'S FAN

ACT I

SUMMARY

The scene is set in Lord Windermere's luxurious London house. It is late afternoon. This evening, Lord and Lady Windermere will be giving a ball in honor of Lady Windermere's twenty-first birthday.

We see Lady Windermere in the morning room, gracefully arranging roses in a bowl. Her butler (no household on a Wilde play is without one) enters to announce that Lord Darlington has come to call on her. Lord Darlington admires her fan, which her husband has just given her as a birthday present. It has her name written upon it.

From the extravagant flattery with which Lord Darlington addresses Lady Windermere (he talks of covering the street in front of her house with flowers), we sense that he is in love with her. Perhaps Lady Windermere senses it too. Over cups of tea, she reproaches him for the elaborate compliments he has been paying her recently. She says that there is no sense in saying a lot of things one does not mean. He protests that he means every word he says.

It is Lady Windermere's opinion that Lord Darlington is a better man than most, but that he pretends to be bad. He agrees to that; if he were to pretend to be good, he is sure everyone would take him seriously. Since he pretends to be bad, nobody takes him seriously. Now the conversation takes on a more earnest tone. Darlington wants only Lady Windermere to take him seriously. He feels she may someday need a friend, but he refuses to explain this rather ominous statement.

Lady Windermere now talks a bit about her own life - how her mother died when she was very young, and how she was brought up by an aunt who had strict ideas about right and wrong. This, she tells Lord Darlington, is no doubt why she herself has uncompromising standards. She calls herself a Puritan.

Lord Darlington then turns the conversation to immorality and how it should be treated. Suppose, he says, a young husband begins to see a woman other than his wife; he pays her bills, spends time with her. Should not the wife "console herself" with male friends of her own? No, Lady Windermere replies. If a man does wrong, that does not mean that his wife ought to behave the same way.

Darlington brings up another point. If a woman has once sinned, should she ever be forgiven? Again Lady Windermere refuses to compromise. No, she answers, such a woman should never be forgiven. Also, men should be judged by the same rules as women.

> Such black-and-white attitudes, Lord Darlington feels, are unrealistic. Life is too complicated to be judged in this over-simplified way.

Comment

This scene has the dual purpose of setting the scene and supplying necessary information. Elegance and luxury are well suggested, not only by the flowers, the morning room, the butler, and the tea service, but by the ornate style of the conversation.

Much valuable information is provided. The fan, which is important enough in the action to be used as the title of the play, is introduced almost immediately. The fact that today is Lady Windermere's twenty-first birthday is made clear. This establishes her youth; more important, it gives a reason for the ball that will be held in the evening.

We learn too that Lord Darlington is much attracted by Lady Windermere. From his dark hints, we guess that Lord Windermere is involved with another woman who has a doubtful reputation. (We catch his meaning faster than Lady Windermere does.) We gather that Lord Darlington is slowly beginning to undermine Lady Windermere's confidence in her husband, with the hope that she will finally transfer her love to Darlington.

Lady Windermere and Lord Darlington personify two different moral attitudes. Lady Windermere, young and inexperienced, takes an uncompromising stand against immorality. Here, as in almost all Victorian plays, this refers to sexual immorality. Such immorality can never be justified and never excused.

Unlike the "puritan" Lady Windermere, Lord Darlington has a more tolerant and sophisticated attitude. He points out that life is too complex to be judged by simple rules. Also, he makes the point that a puritanical standard of values gives far more importance to evil than it ought to have.

However, while we recognize in Darlington a more experienced attitude to moral questions, we are also aware that at times he comes very close to having no moral values at all. For him, the only sensible standard by which to judge people is whether they are "charming" or "tedious." This makes his efforts to win Lady Windermere from her husband more sinister. We are made to feel that no moral restraints will hold him back.

Lord Darlington is a practiced and amusing conversationalist. His speech is ornamented with epigrams (an epigram is a witty thought, cleverly expressed); for example: "I can resist everything but temptation."

SUMMARY

The Duchess of Berwick and her daughter, Lady Agatha Carlisle, come to call. Soon, Lord Darlington leaves, which causes the Duchess to explain how very much she likes him and how glad she is that he is gone.

The Duchess now sets her dutiful daughter to looking at photograph albums and admiring the sunset so that she can be quite alone with Lady Windermere. She sympathizes with Lady Windermere over her misfortune. Lady Windermere, not realizing that she has suffered any misfortune, is bewildered. With a good deal of relish, the Duchess explains that Lord Windermere has been seen several times each week visiting a Mrs. Erlynne, a woman whose reputation is so bad that she is not received in society at all. It would also seem that he is paying Mrs. Erlynne's bills.

The Duchess is also distressed because her own brother, Lord Augustus Lorton, is infatuated with Mrs. Erlynne. The Duchess has advice for Lady Windermere: she should take her husband away from England. This will give him a chance to forget his unfortunate infatuation. The Duchess speaks from long experience; the Duke, her husband, seems to be a very susceptible man.

The Duchess and Lady Agatha now leave. Lady Windermere is left alone with this upsetting information.

Comment

Before he leaves, Lord Darlington has the opportunity to create a few new epigrams. It is amusing to see that he confuses the Duchess of Berwick completely. To his remark that "life is far too important a thing ever to talk seriously about it," she responds frankly that she has no idea what he is talking about.

But of course the main purpose of the scene is to permit Lady Windermere to find out about the suspicious relationship between her husband and Mrs. Erlynne. The Duchess of Berwick is really nothing but a very dull plot element - the third party who brings necessary information. Wilde has cleverly turned her into a delightful joke as well, as she chats about life and love with a mixture of absurdity and hard cynicism.

The superb touch which caps the scene is Lady Agatha. Her mother talks to her and about her throughout; she herself never says more than "Yes, mamma." The Duchess describes a young Australian, very rich, who is much interested in Agatha. Her mother is of the opinion that this Mr. Hopper is "attracted by dear Agatha's clever talk."

Although they are not among the main characters, the Duchess of Berwick and Lady Agatha Carlisle are high points in the play. This is characteristic of Wilde's earlier plays: the incidental characters are more interesting than those around whom the main plot is woven.

SUMMARY

After the Duchess of Berwick leaves with her daughter, Lady Windermere decides to investigate her husband's bankbook to see whether what she has been told is true. She hesitates for a moment, but her feelings are too strong for her. She takes the book from the desk drawer; there is nothing in it about money paid to Mrs. Erlynne. However, she then finds a second bankbook, which is locked. She cuts it open. Her worst fears come true - the book records many large payments to Mrs. Erlynne.

Lord Windermere enters. He reproaches his wife for opening his bankbook. She in turn is bitter over his infatuation with another woman. He denies absolutely that he has any dishonorable relationship with Mrs. Erlynne. He adds that he wants to ask a favor of his wife. Will she invite Mrs. Erlynne to her birthday ball? He explains that Mrs. Erlynne made a great mistake twenty years ago when she was very young and has been an outcast from society ever since. If a woman of high reputation, such as Lady

Windermere, will receive her, she may become acceptable in respectable circles once more.

Lady Windermere feels that she is being put in the intolerable position of publicly receiving her husband's mistress in her own home. She is naturally enraged. She refuses to send Mrs. Erlynne an invitation. When his pleas have no effect, Lord Windermere finally writes the invitation and sends it himself. His wife vows that if Mrs. Erlynne comes, she will strike her across the face with her fan - the one she has just received for a birthday present. She then goes to her room until the party begins. Left alone, Lord Windermere expresses his desperation - and his fear that his wife will find out who Mrs. Erlynne really is.

Comment

The last part of Act I is a good example of Wilde's skillful handling of conventional melodrama. Like Scribe, he gets every possible bit of suspense and excitement out of the plot situation. For example, the first bankbook Lady Windermere looks at is innocent, but then she finds a second one that confirms her suspicions. Then too, the more Lord Windermere talks about Mrs. Erlynne's past life, the surer we become that she must be the mother that Lady Windermere believes to be dead. (Our belief is proved correct by Lord Windermere's final words in this act.) Thus the action ends on a note of high suspense. Will Lady Windermere insult Mrs. Erlynne when she comes to the ball? Will she unwittingly abuse her own mother?

Once again, Lady Windermere's narrow, inflexible ideas are stressed. Both Lord Darlington and the Duchess have already made mention of her high standards. Now her husband remarks that she has a hardness in her nature that seems to go along with her being a good woman. She is not made ashamed or uneasy by his words. She does not stop to examine her own attitude; she is positive that she is right. Before the play is over, Lady Windermere will find that she does not know nearly as much about life as she thinks. She will have to revise her ideas of what is right and what is wrong.

We do not see Mrs. Erlynne in Act I; however, we do get some **foreshadowing** of her character. If she can force her son-in-law to pay her large sums of money, if she can make him get her an invitation to the ball in spite of Lady Windermere's frantic opposition, she must be both strong and unscrupulous. What she is doing amounts to blackmail.

ACT II

SUMMARY

> The ball is in progress. The house is full of lights and flowers. Guests are constantly arriving-some that we recognize and some whom we have not yet met. The Duchess of Berwick is present with her daughter. She checks over Agatha's dance program; she notes with approval that Agatha has saved five dances for Mr. Hopper, the rich, eligible young Australian. She crosses out the names of a couple of young men; they are younger sons and therefore will not inherit much family property. The submissive Agatha has nothing to say except "Yes, mamma."

Lord Darlington arrives. He is attentive to Lady Windermere, as usual. Mr. Hopper comes and is enthusiastically greeted by the Duchess. Other people join the party-Lady Plymdale; her attentive escort, Mr. Dumby; socially prominent Lady Jedburgh; Lord Augustus Lorton, brother to the Duchess of Berwick, who seems to be infatuated with Mrs. Erlynne; Cecil Graham, a cynical young man about town who is a nephew of Lady Jedburgh.

At last, Mrs. Erlynne herself arrives. There is a moment of suspense: Lady Windermere clutches her fan. But that moment passes without incident. Lady Windermere cannot bring herself to create a public scene. At Mrs. Erlynne's insistence, Lord Windermere dances with her. Lord Augustus is made to propose by this strategy. By the end of the evening, Mrs. Erlynne is a stunning social success. Lady Jedburgh even issues a luncheon invitation.

Lady Agatha has somehow gotten engaged to Mr. Hopper. And, as many of the guests leave, Mrs. Erlynne once more captures Lord Windermere - this time to ask for a substantial cash settlement, enough so that she can bring to her new husband an income of pounds 2,500 ($12,500, with a purchasing power many times what it has in our day).

To Lady Windermere, the evening has seemed to be a purposeful public humiliation of her by Mrs. Erlynne and her husband. Lord Darlington takes advantage of her suffering. He tells her that he loves her and begs her to come away with him. She refuses. But when she sees her husband going out on the terrace with Mrs. Erlynne (she cannot guess what an unromantic business conference this really is), she can endure no more. Lord Darlington is gone, however; he has decided to leave England in the morning. She writes a note to her husband which explains what she intends to do, and then leaves for Darlington's home.

Mrs. Erlynne finds her note. Guessing what has happened she opens the note. Her fears are true. To her surprise, Mrs. Erlynne finds that somewhere inside her there is love for this daughter whom she has not seen since babyhood. She will try to save her from making the same terrible mistake as her mother. Mrs. Erlynne orders the bewildered Lord Augustus to take Lord Windermere to his club and keep him there for the rest of the night. (The way must be kept clear for Lady Windermere to return to the house without her husband's knowledge.) Mrs. Erlynne then prepares to follow Lady Windermere to Lord Darlington's home.

Comment

The ballroom scene is handled in an accomplished manner. Many people come in and out. Snatches of conversation are overheard. They are enough to characterize the speakers sharply-for example, Lady Jedburgh is imperious, Mr. Dumby is amiably stupid, Cecil Graham is a cynical egotist. Small subplots are developed and concluded: Lady Plymdale is furiously jealous when she learns that Mr. Dumby has been flirting with Mrs. Erlynne, but on second thought she feels that Mrs. Erlynne will attract Lord Plymdale, her husband-a most useful arrangement, since it will leave Lady Plymdale free to live her own life as she pleases.

The romance of Lady Agatha and Mr. Hopper is brought to a **climax** in this act. A few dances and a tete-a-tete on the terrace lead Mr. Hopper to propose to the "little chatterbox," as her mother calls her. The Duchess' manner toward Mr. Hopper changes most amusingly after the proposal. She is all honeyed sweetness before, expressing her interest in Australia, "with all the dear little kangaroos flying about." After all is over, Australia becomes "that dreadful, vulgar place." The worst feature seems to be "horrid kangaroos crawling about." She refuses to hear of Agatha going there to live. No word passes Agatha's lips except "Yes, mamma."

The Duchess' conversation is full of remarks which seem to have a logical character but which really make no sense at all. For example, talking about Australia as it appears on the map, she says: "What a curious shape it is! Just like a large packing case! However, it is a very young country, isn't it?" This implies that somehow when Australia is older and wiser it will change its shape to a more desirable one. Pseudo-logical remarks which are actually wild nonsense are an important part of Wilde's comic technique. He developed great skill in their use by the time he wrote *The Importance of Being Earnest* (1895). (See The Plays.)

Mrs. Erlynne is a most effective figure in this act. She shows personal force and social adroitness as she forces Windermere to dance attendance upon her, makes Lord Augustus jealous, soothes the Duchess of Berwick, and flatters Lady Jedburgh. There is also a certain courageous humor about her. Now that she is about to succeed in her ruthless drive to be received once more in good society, she can look at the situation with amusement.

Once again, the suspense is artfully created. At the beginning, we wait tensely to discover whether Lady Windermere will carry out her threat and strike Mrs. Erlynne with her fan. This crisis over, uncertainty is created concerning whether Lady Windermere will succumb to Lord Darlington and run away with him. Finally, we are caught up in Mrs. Erlynne's effort to save Lady Windermere. With this last crisis at its height, the act ends.

ACT III

SUMMARY

The scene is Lord Darlington's "rooms" (what we would call his apartment). Lady Windermere is waiting there alone. She wavers between staying and going back home, in an agony of indecision. She has just made up her mind to go when Mrs. Erlynne enters and demands that she return home at once. Lady Windermere is convinced that her husband has sent Mrs. Erlynne to bring her back; he would like to avoid an open scandal, she believes, and use her as cover for his relationship with Mrs. Erlynne. Mrs. Erlynne swears that Lord Windermere does not even know that his wife is out of the house. She confesses that she opened Lady Windermere's note. She even holds it up for Lady Windermere to see; then she throws it into the fire. But Lady Windermere does not have a chance to examine the note closely, and she still does not believe Mrs. Erlynne.

Mrs. Erlynne now tells her from her own experience what the life of an outcast from society is like. She also assures her that Lord Windermere loves his wife. She reminds her of her duty to her little child, only six months old. Lady Windermere is moved. She is about to leave with Mrs. Erlynne when the voices of the men are heard outside. Mrs. Erlynne tells Lady Windermere to hide behind a curtain and slip out if there is a chance. She herself flees into the next room. Unfortunately, Lady Windermere forgets to take her fan.

Lord Darlington enters. With him are Mr. Dumby Cecil Graham, and Lord Augustus Lorton who, still obeying Mrs. Erlynne's instructions, is in the company of the somewhat tired and puzzled Lord Windermere. Cecil Graham and Mr. Dumby tease Lord Augustus over his attachment to Mrs. Erlynne.

Lord Darlington admits he himself is in love. He loves a good woman, and she has changed him entirely. Meanwhile, Cecil Graham has found the fan. He is amused to think that Darlington has a woman in his rooms at the same time that he has been talking of the nobility of his new-found love. He shows the fan first to Lord Augustus and then to Lord Windermere. Lord Windermere recognizes it. He demands an explanation and threatens to search Darlington's rooms. He is about to start his search with the curtain behind which his wife is hidden when Mrs. Erlynne enters the room. She says that she took the fan by mistake when she left the Windermeres' house. In the confusion, Lady Windermere slips out unseen.

Comment

In this act, Lady Windermere and Mrs. Erlynne really confront one another for the first time though they are linked together by their destiny and by their secret relationship. They have a chance to examine one another closely. Mrs. Erlynne finds that her daughter is weak and defenseless and must be protected.

Lady Windermere is angry and suspicious, but she is impressed at last by the older woman's sincerity and strength. Mrs. Erlynne finds herself making a sacrifice of her own future for the sake of her daughter. (When Lord Augustus sees her in Darlington's rooms, it is most unlikely that he will marry her.)

The conversation of the men about life and love contains some of Wilde's most characteristic writing. Cecil Graham, particularly, seems to speak with Wilde's own voice. When Darlington speaks of the purity and innocence men have lost, Graham retorts: "My dear fellow, what on earth should we men do going about with purity and innocence? A carefully thought out buttonhole [i.e., flower in the buttonhole] is much more effective." However, the other men also have striking epigrams to deliver. Lord Darlington defines a cynic: "A man who knows the price of everything and the value of nothing." Dumby remarks: "Experience is the name everyone gives to their mistakes."

Notice the skill with which the scene is constructed. Mrs. Erlynne and Lady Windermere are paired together. So are Windermere and Darlington. Neither pair of characters has spoken together extensively till now, though their lives are entangled with one another. Their relationships even have a sort of parallelism: the wife and presumed mistress of the same man, and the husband and the would-be lover of the same woman.

Like the first two acts, this one ends at a high point. But in this case we have a **climax** rather than a moment of suspense. Lady Windermere is saved; Mrs. Erlynne appears to be ruined.

ACT IV

SUMMARY

It is the next morning. We see Lady Windermere alone in the morning-room. She has not seen her husband yet, so that she is not sure whether Mrs. Erlynne has protected her or has broken down and told the truth. She feels that if her husband does not know the truth about last night, she will have to tell him herself.

Lord Windermere enters. He greets her lovingly; clearly, he has no idea that she was ever at Darlington's rooms. He tells her that Mrs. Erlynne is a much worse woman than he thought; therefore, Lady Windermere is never to see her again. But Lady Windermere has learned much from last night's experience. She no longer has confidence in the simple epithets, "good" and "bad." She is aware that all people (even herself!) have possibilities in both directions. She defends Mrs. Erlynne and when that lady calls to return her fan, she insists upon inviting her up.

Mrs. Erlynne reveals that she is leaving England permanently. She asks Lady Windermere for a photograph of herself and her baby. While she is getting it, Lord Windermere and Mrs. Erlynne have the opportunity for a private conversation.

Windermere speaks bitterly of her immorality, and of her conscienceless blackmailing of him; she has understood that Windermere would do anything so that his wife might be saved from knowing that Mrs. Erlynne is her mother, and she has heartlessly taken advantage of that fact. He forbids

> her ever to see her daughter again. He says he will tell his wife the truth. Mrs. Erlynne forbids him to; she will decide herself whether Lady Windermere is to be told.

Comment

This act contains several ironical twists. We see Lord Windermere attacking Mrs. Erlynne and Lady Windermere defending her, a startling reversal of their positions in Act I. Lord Windermere now wants to keep her out of the house, and Lady Windermere wants to receive her.

Also, the act begins with Lord Windermere afraid that Mrs. Erlynne is going to tell her daughter who she is. Later, he reverses himself; he decides he will tell his wife the truth, for this is the safer path of action. It will be less painful for her if he tells her than if she finds out in another way. Thus, the suspense is kept up steadily. We are not certain until the very end of the play whether Lady Windermere will learn about her mother.

There are some sentimental elements in the portrait of Mrs. Erlynne: the mother's heart that beats within that sophisticated exterior betrays her. She suffers, and she becomes unselfish. But Wilde still manages to preserve the impression of cool, amused self-possession that she gives during much of the play. She cannot resist exasperating her son-in-law. She treats him with good-natured contempt. She refuses to repent her misdeeds; repentance requires the wearing of ugly clothes to be really convincing, she says, and she certainly will not consider that; she expresses surprise that her son-in-law could dream of her doing such a thing. She is leaving, but she plans to enjoy herself as much as possible.

SUMMARY

Lady Windermere now returns with the picture, and Mrs. Erlynne encourages her to talk about her parents. Lady Windermere shows that she idolizes her mother. When she begins to speak of how brokenhearted her father was over her mother's death, Mrs. Erlynne can bear no more and gets up to go. She obviously is going to keep her secret. Lord Windermere goes out, to see whether Mrs. Erlynne's carriage is outside.

While the two women are alone, Mrs. Erlynne makes Lady Windermere promise that she will never tell her husband about the night before. Lord Windermere soon returns. Mrs. Erlynne asks for, and is given, the fan to keep.

As she is about to leave, Lord Augustus comes to call. He is cold toward Mrs. Erlynne, but she skillfully forces him to escort her outside to her carriage. The Windermeres pledge renewed love and trust to one another. Lord Augustus returns, in a joyful mood-Mrs. Erlynne has explained about her presence in Lord Darlington's rooms. (Explaining seems to be one of her talents; she has explained away numerous embarrassing incidents to Lord Augustus in the past.) She went there to find Lord Augustus and accept his proposal of marriage. They are now definitely engaged. To the relief of Lord Windermere, they plan to live abroad after their marriage.

Comment

The play is finished off in a neat manner. Lady Windermere has become mature and tolerant. Lord Windermere is freed of his burden of fear and blackmail. Mrs. Erlynne will leave the scene where she has disturbed so many lives. She too has learned some lessons. And she is rewarded for her good deed; her alliance with Lord Augustus (who is socially desirable if not too bright) is not ruined after all.

Thus we may say in summary that the play is assembled in an efficient manner. It contains the ingredients of comedy, sentiment, and suspense in nice proportions. The characters cavort in consciously effective entrances and exits. No one of them dominates the play enough to disturb its balance. Their scenes with one another are varied and well arranged. For example, Lady Windermere has a major scene with her husband, a major scene with Lord Darlington, and a major scene with Mrs. Erlynne, as well as a couple of soliloquies.

It may be objected that the play is rather contrived, that the language and situations do not create a sense of genuine human experience. These objections certainly have validity. They apply to the majority of plays written in this manner - "well-made plays" as they are sometimes called. Wilde has merely written a play like many other plays of this type. He handles the story well, but without great conviction. It is hard to believe that he cares much about the Windermeres. But in minor figures such as the Duchess, Lady Agatha, Mr. Dumby, and Cecil Graham, Wilde displays his original gifts - and his promise for the future.

CHARACTERIZATIONS

Mrs. Erlynne: This is by far the most successful character study in the play. Mrs. Erlynne is a calculating woman who has been forced for many years to live by her wits. She has the conventional characteristics that this sort of part usually demands: she finds that she has not really escaped human feelings and she makes a great personal sacrifice for her daughter. But, more important, she manages to give just the impression that the author intends: she has a relish for life that makes her enjoy her intrigues; and she seems to have by far the most powerful intelligence and forceful personality in the play.

Lady Windermere: The change in Lady Windermere's character is perhaps the main **theme** of the play. At the beginning, she is absolutely sure of herself and her ideas. She has been strictly brought up by her aunt, and she is very young. She feels no pity for anyone who sins against the moral code; the sinner must be punished. She can feel no sympathy for a wrongdoer because she is so positive that she herself could never do wrong. It does not occur to her that there is something unrealistic in this attitude.

But when a series of circumstances bring her to within a hair's breadth of becoming a sinner and an outcast herself, she learns to have some merciful feelings towards the sinner. Also, the sinner is capable of goodness, as she learns when Mrs. Erlynne protects her from her own foolishness by an act of self-sacrifice. At the end of the play, Lady Windermere has made progress as a human being. She has learned to be more realistic in her judgments.

Unfortunately, it is difficult to portray a character who is both intolerant and appealing. Lady Windermere gives a somewhat priggish impression.

Lord Windermere: He is a good man who loves his wife deeply. He is most uncomfortably under Mrs. Erlynne's control for most of the play, and it is his part to react rather than act.

Trapped by Mrs. Erlynne, he is furious because of this. He is wretched at his wife's unjustified suspicions of his faithfulness. But he does not have a well-defined character of his own.

Lord Darlington: In the first two acts, Lord Darlington acts like a man practiced in the art of seduction. He pays flattering attention to a young married woman of innocent nature. He begins to plant suspicions against her husband in her mind. When she is confused and defenseless, he makes a passionate declaration of his love and begs her to run away with him. But later our view of him changes. From what he says to his friends, he is genuinely in love with Lady Windermere. This is apparently because she is a good woman: she has withstood him and stayed faithful to her marriage vows. He states that he is a changed man because of her. Presumably, he leaves England still suffering from his hopeless, idealistic passion, for we do not hear of him again after Act III.

Lord Augustus Lorton: He is talkative, impressionable, foolish-a dithering aristocrat of the kind later made famous in the comic novels of P. G. Wodehouse.

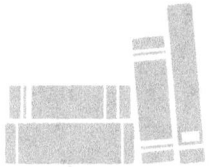

A WOMAN OF NO IMPORTANCE

ACT I

SUMMARY

The scene is Hunstanton Chase, a large English country house. There is a house party in progress. On the lawn, several of the guests are in conversation. There is Hester Worsley, an American girl, rich and pretty, and also Sir John and Lady Caroline Pontefract. They are joined by Lady Hunstanton, their hostess, and then by Gerald Arbuthnot, a young man who works as a clerk in a bank. Gerald brings good news. Lord Illingworth, an influential man who is also staying at the house, has offered him the position of his private secretary. Gerald and Hester go off for a walk.

Mrs. Allonby and Lady Stutfield now enter. Lady Stutfield is an excessively amiable lady who agrees enthusiastically with every idea she hears. Mrs. Allonby is witty and sophisticated. Her reputation is not good. Lady Caroline says at one point (before Mrs. Allonby is present) that there is a story that Mrs. Allonby ran away twice (presumably with young men) before she was married. However, Lady Caroline discounts the gossip; she feels sure it was only once.

Mr. Kelvil arrives next. He is a member of Parliament who writes and talks constantly about the importance of purity (i.e., sexual morality) in modern life. Next comes Lord Illingworth, whose evil reputation has preceded him in the play. Lady Stutfield greets him with an arch, flirtatious remark about what a wicked man he is. Lord Illingworth, the very picture of worldliness and wit, does not deny it.

There is general chatter. Mr. Kelvil and Lord Illingworth have a brief political discussion. Mr. Kelvil mentions the sufferings of the poor. Lord Illingworth disapproves of such talk; poverty is ugly, and the less said about ugly things, the better. Only beauty and joy deserve attention.

The party goes inside the house for tea. Lord Illinoworth and Mrs. Allonby are the last to go. Mrs. Allonby shows her dislike to Hester Worsley, whom she calls a Puritan. Lord Illingworth boasts that he could kiss Hester and Hester would like it. Mrs. Allonby is skeptical.

Lord Illingworth notices a note on the table. It happens to be from Mrs. Arbuthnot, Gerald's mother, telling Lady Hunstanton she will visit after dinner. He remarks on the handwriting; it reminds him of a handwriting he used to know. "Whose?" asks Mrs. Allonby. Lord Illingworth replies carelessly that it was a woman of no importance.

Comment

When we consider Act I in terms of plot, we observe that virtually nothing happens. The important fact which emerges is that Lord Illingworth is about to make Gerald Arbuthnot his secretary. Besides that, we learn about the relationships between the characters - that Mrs. Allonby and Hester Worsley dislike one another (Mrs. Allonby being corrupt and "modern," Hester being young and decent); we learn that Lady Caroline Pontefract directs her husband's every move and makes it her special care to protect him from attractive women; we observe that Lord Illingworth and Mrs. Allonby carry on a constant and very talkative flirtation.

But there is little momentum or excitement. It is especially noteworthy that the ending of the act is comparatively tame. There is no suspense, no crisis, nothing to make the audience wait anxiously for Act II. The pace, variety, and suspense we find in Act I of *Lady Windermere's Fan* are absent here. The act ends with the mildly interesting suggestion that Lord Illingworth has known Mrs. Arbuthnot long ago.

The minor characters are an amusing set of caricatures. Conscientious Mr. Kelvil, with his praises of family life, while his wife and eight children are conveniently distant at a seaside resort, is cleverly sketched. However, he has practically no further dialogue in the play. He amounts only to a short comedy act. Lady Stutfield has no mind of her own. Her characteristic speech mannerism is the double emphatic ("very, very glad," "so, so sad," etc.), which suggests gushing earnestness and intellectual flabbiness at the same time.

Lady Hunstanton's is perhaps the most successful small portrait. Her characteristic habit is forgetfulness, but the way she forgets is entirely her own. For example, she remarks that there was a lady whom Lord Illingworth was thinking of marrying, but "her family was too large. Or was it her feet? I forget which."

The more important characters emerge less successfully. Lord Illingworth and Mrs. Allonby converse almost entirely in epigrams, and while each produces an occasional remark that is witty, or striking, or funny, the general effect is slow, self-conscious, and obscure.

For example, Lord Illingworth remarks: "I never intend to grow old. The soul is born old but grows young. That is the comedy of life." Mrs. Allonby replies: "And the body is born young and grows old. That is life's tragedy." The two remarks are carefully constructed to be in opposition to one another. However, the first one does not have a very clear meaning, while the second one is crudely obvious.

But we must also note the successes, for Wilde cannot write a series of epigrams without producing an occasional gem, such as Lord Illingworth's characterization of the Englishman chasing the fox during the hunt - "the unspeakable in full pursuit of the uneatable."

Some attempt has been made to characterize Lord Illingworth in a solid manner. He is cynical and conscienceless in his relations with women, like all bad noblemen in Victorian literature. But his views on life are distinctive. He has no room for pity and no inclination to help the unfortunate, because poverty and suffering are ugly. He wants no ugliness in his life. He confines his reactions to beauty, color, and joy. It would almost seem as if Lord Illingworth has been influenced by the views of Water Pater (see Introduction). The love of beauty, divorced from ethical responsibility, is characteristic of the aesthetic movement - the movement of which Oscar Wilde was such an important part. The most wicked and unsympathetic character in the play has been made by Wilde into a virtual portrait of himself. If suggests that he enjoyed parading his opposition to conventional ideas, but at the same time he recognized the faults and weaknesses of this outlook.

ACT II

SUMMARY

It is after dinner. The ladies are in the drawing-room at Hunstanton Chase. They have left the men in the dining-room to enjoy coffee, cigars, and brandy, as is the English custom. Mrs. Allonby contributes many cynical remarks to the conversation, including contemptuous references to her own husband, as well as a lengthy description of how a woman likes to be treated by her lover. (As Lady Caroline Pontefract puts it, "he is to do nothing but pay bills and compliments.")

Hester Worsley has listened to the conversation without comment. Now she rises and delivers a burning denunciation of English society, calling it heartless and immoral. She contrasts it with American society, which glorifies virtue and industry and has no sympathy with snobbish class distinctions. She makes bitter comments about one Sir Henry Weston, a wicked man who is gladly received in the best society while the many women he has ruined are social outcasts. (This leads to an embarrassing moment, when it turns out that Sir Henry Weston is Lady Caroline's brother.)

Mrs. Arbuthnot comes in during this tirade. She seems personally affected by Hester's remarks about ruined women. She learns from her hostess that Lord Illingworth succeeded to the family title only a few years ago; before that he was plain George Harford. Again she is upset.

The men now join the ladies. Mrs. Allonby is still unhealthily occupied with the idea of Lord Illingworth making love to Hester. She challenges him, and he makes a private wager with her that he can do it within a week.

Gerald is full of naive admiration for Lord Illingworth's wisdom and experience. Over her objections he insists on introducing Lord Illingworth to his mother. It is Lord Illingworth's turn to be startled. Mrs. Arbuthnot is coldly polite. She raises objections to the secretaryship; she states that Gerald is not qualified for the position.

Now Lady Hunstanton shepherds her guests into the music room, where Hester is going to entertain them with a violin solo. Lord Illingworth stays behind to discuss Gerald's career with Mrs. Arbuthnot.

As soon as they are alone, it is clear that he once seduced her and Gerald is their son. She recalls how, encouraged by his doting mother, he refused to marry her and give his child a legitimate name. She swears she will not let Gerald fall under his influence. Illingworth is coolly firm. After all these years, he wants his son. He liked Gerald before he realized the relationship. Now he certainly wants to have him near. Mrs. Arbuthnot begs him to leave her the boy; he is all she has. Illingworth is untouched by this appeal. When Gerald returns to the room, his mother can only offer feeble

> objections. She cannot explain the real reason she does not want him to go with Lord Illingworth. It is finally settled that Gerald will go.

Comment

The plot now begins to exhibit features very familiar in Victorian plays. There is a scene of recognition between a wronged woman and her seducer. She is grieving and bitter, while he is full of villainous sneers. He exhibits no remorse for his misdeeds. They fight for the destiny of their child; she, the good influence, is tongue-tied and helpless, while he, the evil influence, is full of false glamour. However, they have no human depth. Their feelings do not move the reader or audience; their speeches are wildly exaggerated and artificial, a circumstance that will grow more pronounced as the play proceeds. It is impossible to believe in them.

Hester is cut from the same cardboard as the others. The effect that Wilde intends to produce with her fails seriously. She is meant to be noble and courageous, the voice of truth which shatters false values. Unfortunately, she seems smug and priggish instead, and one is struck by her poor manners rather than by her nobility.

Mrs. Allonby's remarks on love and marriage are not only questionable. They are long-winded-a new and fatal error for Wilde to make. Mrs. Erlynne is not half so talkative, and she is more amusing; we have far more belief in her clever wickedness.

Act II is enlivened by the introduction of the local clergyman, Doctor Daubeny. His wife (who is constantly talked about but never appears) seems to be in the process of total disintegration. She suffers from headaches, deafness, and failing eyesight, but Doctor Daubeny is absolutely saintly in the way he bears up under his wife's afflictions. He never worries about her. He is quite sure that she is perfectly happy.

Once again, undistinguished melodrama is somewhat redeemed by Wilde's gay and extravagant caricature of a minor character.

ACT III

SUMMARY

The time is immediately after the last scene. Lord Illingworth and Gerald are having a cigarette together. Lord Illingworth is busy at his task of educating the young man. That is, he is expanding his own influence over him, filling him with worldly ideas, and delicately proceeding to alienate him from his mother.

He talks wittily of the importance of skillful dinner-table conversation and a well-tied necktie. He gives Gerald hints on the handling of women, sneers at the female sex ("women represent the triumph of matter over mind"), and is contemptuous of marriage and romance. Mrs. Arbuthnot is the best of women, but of course, he adds, she does not understand the needs and ambitions of a grown son. She is selfish in her love, wishing her son to live as narrow and restricted a life as she does. She is more interested in going to church than in fine clothes and fashionable society-a hopelessly out-of-date attitude.

They are interrupted by the return of the rest of the party, who join the discussion. Lady Hunstanton confesses once more her inability to understand what Lord Illingworth is talking about. Dr. Daubeny leaves, for his wife's health is always bad on Tuesdays. He reveals that her memory has failed, and she lives entirely on jellies, being unable to eat any solid food. However, he is very cheerful and philosophical about all these afflictions. Now most of the party exit, and Lord Illingworth accompanies Mrs. Allonby on a visit to the terrace to look at the stars; Gerald goes along.

Hester comes in to speak to Mrs. Arbuthnot, who is alone. Hester begs her to prevent her son from going with Lord Illingworth. Hester goes out to the terrace and sends Gerald in to his mother.

Mrs. Arbuthnot urges her son passionately not to go with Lord Illingworth. Gerald becomes angry. He cannot understand why his mother tries to interfere with his remarkable opportunity to begin a fine career. He states that all she has taught him about the world, society, and success is wrong. Lord Illingworth has convinced him that worldly success is indeed worth having. He hopes to be just like Lord Illingworth. These last words make Mrs. Arbuthnot desperate. She tells him of Lord Illingworth's heartless seduction of an eighteen-year-old girl twenty years ago. She does not reveal that the girl was herself. Gerald is not particularly horrified. He says that no doubt it was the girl's fault as much as the man's; she could not have been a really nice girl!

His mother is heartbroken by these words. Lord Illingworth has said to her that her son loves her now, but will eventually judge her. His prophecy has come true. She withdraws all her objections.

Gerald is just expressing his pleasure at this when Hester runs into the room and throws herself into his arms, begging for protection from Lord Illingworth. Lord Illingworth has chosen this moment to try to win his bet and has just forced a kiss upon Hester. Gerald is enraged; he wants to kill the offender. His mother is not strong enough to hold him back. At last she tells him that the man he wants to kill is really his father. Then she sinks to the floor, overcome by shame. Hester tactfully withdraws, and Gerald helps his mother to rise and leads her home.

ACT IV

SUMMARY

The scene is now in the sitting-room of Mrs. Arbuthnot's home-what Mrs. Allonby will describe sarcastically as "quite the happy English home." That is, it is pretty, with flowers, books, and pictures, none of which is exotic or shocking.

Mrs. Allonby and Lady Hunstanton come to call on Mrs. Arbuthnot. (It is the morning after the violent scene which climaxes Act III.) Mrs. Arbuthnot sends down a message explaining that she has a headache and cannot see them. Gerald tells them that he plans to refuse Lord Illingworth's offer and stay with his mother. Lady Hunstanton urges him to change his mind. She and Mrs. Allonby then leave.

Mrs. Arbuthnot enters. Gerald tells her that he has just finished writing a letter to Lord Illingworth. The letter demands that Lord Illingworth marry Gerald's mother.

Gerald is thunderstruck when Mrs. Arbuthnot absolutely refuses to consider such a marriage. He cannot understand how she can refuse to marry the father of her child. She explains that to go through the sacrament of marriage in a church with the man she loathes would be lying to God.

Still Gerald protests that he cannot understand his mother's attitude. She now proceeds, in the longest speech in the play, to explain herself. She describes at great length the pains of motherhood - the physical danger of bearing a child, the struggle to raise it to maturity, the child's unconscious cruelty and ingratitude. She tells how Gerald made friends and enjoyed himself in other people's houses, where she could not go because of her secret shame. Instead, she went among the poor and sick and performed works of charity, for they did not care about her past. Yet, she says, in spite of the disappointments of motherhood, she has never for a moment regretted having Gerald. Her love for him has been so great that she has been unable to repent her sin: it was the sin that gave him to her.

Still Gerald insists that it is her duty to marry Lord Illingworth. But Hester rushes in from where she has been listening and passionately defends Mrs. Arbuthnot. She states that to marry Lord Illingworth would be real dishonor. She asks Mrs. Arbuthnot to come back to America with her. Gerald is bewildered; he does not know what to do. He asks Hester to direct him. She tries to make him understand that if Lord Illingworth is so contemptible that Gerald had to save her from him, it is wrong to demand that his mother marry him. At last, Gerald understands and begs his mother's forgiveness. When she is still hurt and distant with him he flings himself down on the sofa and sobs.

Hester persuades Mrs. Arbuthnot to relent towards Gerald. She reveals that she loves Gerald, poor and outcast though he may be. The three of them plan to leave England together, and never be separated. Hester and Gerald go out into the garden together, Mrs. Arbuthnot tactfully promising to join them later.

While Mrs. Arbuthnot is alone Lord Illingworth comes to see her. He has come to propose an arrangement. Gerald is to stay with him for six months of the year. He will leave Gerald his property, and he will also give Mrs. Arbuthnot a substantial allowance. Mrs. Arbuthnot tells him that Gerald's future is already taken care of. She points into the garden and shows him Gerald and Hester together.

Lord Illingworth notices the letter Gerald has written to him. Though Mrs. Arbuthnot objects, he reads it. He offers to marry her, as Gerald asks, if this will give him his son. She refuses. As he bids her goodbye, he reflects ironically that it was most amusing to visit a house and find there his mistress and his _____. But before Lord Illingworth can bring out the word that would shame Gerald, Mrs. Arbuthnot strikes him across the face with his glove. He leaves, and she falls sobbing on the sofa.

Gerald and Hester return. The two women head for the garden with their arms around each other's waists. Gerald

> notices Lord Illingworth's glove; he asks who has been visiting, to which Mrs. Arbuthnot replies: "A man of no importance."

Comment

Of Oscar Wilde's plays, *A Woman of No Importance* is the one modern readers find hardest to respect and admire; the fourth act is the one of which this is particularly true. It is worth examining Act IV carefully to find out why this is so.

Probably the main reason why we cannot take it seriously is that its values are outdated. We do not have the same ideas as Wilde's audience did, even though only about seventy years separate us-a short time in human history. To a modern reader, the emotional aura that surrounds Mrs. Arbuthnot's twenty-year-old indiscretion seems inappropriate. We may have quite conventional standards of human conduct. We may disapprove of sexual license and illegitimate children as much as our ancestors. Yet for her mistake to be the focal point of Mrs. Arbuthnot's existence, for it to have control over Gerald and Hester, seems unintelligent. It represents too much human waste. Looking backward in perpetual breast-beating remorse seems like an unproductive way to spend one's life.

For the same reason, the three main characters do not have the same values for us that they had in Wilde's day. Wilde meant to portray a self-sacrificing woman who had wiped out her sin by devoted motherhood and constant goodness. Hester is meant to be a sympathetic, fine young woman who appreciates all that Gerald's mother has been through and is therefore able to help Gerald love and understand his mother. Gerald is a young man who has been saved from the path of evil by the love of two good women.

But our twentieth-century viewpoint causes us to see them differently. To us, Mrs. Arbuthnot's preoccupation with her sin seems almost like monomania. Her praise of her own nobility and her complaints over her sad life come close to self-pity. To a generation which has grown up with a suspicion of possessive mothers who like to make their sons feel guilty whenever possible, Mrs. Arbuthnot looks like a rather dangerous woman.

Wilde's portrait of Gerald, unfortunately, reinforces this opinion. Mrs. Arbuthnot tells Lord Illingworth at one point that she has brought Gerald up to be a good man. The play hints that she has brought him up to be simple-minded. He seems weak-willed, naive, and unduly influenced by his mother. This influence is reinforced by his wife-to-be. At the end of the play, Gerald strolls out into the garden with the wife and mother who love him. The three of them hope never to be separated. To a twentieth-century reader, it looks as though poor Gerald is strolling into a future where he will have two women telling him what to do instead of only one.

Hester has little reality. She probably was not very convincing even in 1893. She is supposed to be an American, which, to an English audience, might have explained why she acted in a way entirely unfamiliar to them. But she is only a mouthpiece for virtuous ideas. She defends democracy against snobbishness. She defends goodness and morality. She mourns the sufferings of Mrs. Arbuthnot, the unwed mother. In doing this, she moderates her biblical position against sexual misbehavior. At the beginning, she feels that all participants should be condemned to the same suffering - the woman, the man, even the innocent children. Later she changes her mind and states that God's law is only love. This is Wilde's only attempt to humanize her. It is unsuccessful; she remains an incredible figure.

As we try to understand the failure of Act IV by modern standards we must also note the extreme sentimentality with which it is written. What do we mean by "sentimentality?" We mean that a highly emotional tone is purposely used in order to arouse the audience (or reader), rather than because the subject deserves it. In Act IV, the dialogue is constantly overexcited. We sense that the author is interested in whipping up our feelings, rather than expressing the truth of the situation. Everything is sacrificed to this highly emotional tone-realism, probability, characterization. The characters speak in a kind of language not heard in real life (Mrs. Arbuthnot's speech on the trials of motherhood is an example), and their reactions are not real human reactions. (When Gerald wants to tell Hester of his love, she orders him away from her, saying, in part: "You cannot honour me unless she's holier to you. In her all womanhood is martyred.") Their feelings are too freely expressed. (Within a very short time, both Gerald and Mrs. Arbuthnot have occasion to fall sobbing on the sofa.) We feel that the author has put us through an emotional wringer for his own purposes.

To summarize, the attitudes and writing methods we find in this play are not convincing. We may even be amused to notice that although the Victorians disapproved sternly of sexual licence they seemed to spend a lot of time thinking and talking about it. The play gives the audience a chance to have all the proper feelings about morality. But while it disapproves of wicked Lord Illingworth and oversophisticated Mrs. Allonby, it also enjoys the opportunity of hearing their witty attacks on conventional ideas. This approach seems basically insincere, and it is therefore difficult to take any part of the play seriously. We need only read the plays of Henrik Ibsen or George Bernard Shaw (see Introduction) for comparison, to see that when a writer has a serious point to make about something he really believes in, the result is quite different. Wilde's examination of sexual standards in *A Woman of No Importance* is superficial and unconvincing.

CHARACTERIZATIONS

Mrs. Arbuthnot

Mrs. Arbuthnot was once an innocent girl of eighteen who was cruelly deceived by a sophisticated young man. He seduced her with the help of false promises of marriage; later, after their child was born, he refused to marry her. We see her twenty years later. Her life is an example to all who know her. (Lady Hunstanton, for instance, is full of admiration for her sweetness and respectability.) She spends her time in works of charity. She has raised her son with devotion and taught him the highest standards of behavior.

Nevertheless, Mrs. Arbuthnot's life is still haunted by her error. She herself says that she knows no real peace or happiness. She refers to herself as a "tainted thing." It is only through Hester's compassion that she finds forgiveness, understanding, and hope for the future.

Gerald

The son of Mrs. Arbuthnot and Lord Illingworth is a pleasant young man who knows little of the great world. He has a fine, upstanding character as a result of his mother's careful training. But in his innocence he is vastly impressed by Lord Illingworth's elegant manner and fine talk, in which wit is substituted for moral standards. Lord Illingworth's behavior toward Hester opens his eyes. Hester's sympathy toward his mother teaches him still more. At the end of the play he has gained enough insight to become a compassionate son and a devoted husband.

Hester Worsley

This young American girl sees the corruption of English society with clear eyes and denounces it courageously. She is especially revolted by what we usually call the double standard of sexual behavior -that is, the female partner in immorality becoming an outcast while the male partner pays no social penalty at all. In her righteousness, she originally feels that both parties should suffer. But compassion teaches her that forgiveness is better than suffering.

Hester is meant as a contrast to Mrs. Allonby, whose character is as doubtful as Hester's is virtuous. She is the straightforward American, the product of a young society whose standards have not had time to deteriorate.

However, it must be added that Hester remains no more than a virtuous symbol in the play. She displays no convincing human trait whatever. Wilde probably did not believe in her himself when he invented her.

Lord Illingworth

This debonaire, immoral man-about-town has many relatives in English literature. Wicked but attractive aristocrats are common in English plays and novels. (See, for example, Thomas Hardy's *Tess of the D'Urbervilles*.) William Gilbert made fun of the type when he wrote about Sir Roderick Murgatroyd, Sir Rupert Murgatroyd, and Sir Ruthven Murtgatroyd, the "bad barts" of the operetta *Ruddigore*. (A "bart" is a baronet, a man whose title of "Sir" is inherited.)

Lord Illingworth is a most amusing conversationalist. He occasionally makes shrewd observations, and he uses language with elegant style. For instance, he remarks to Gerald that to win back youth once more, he would do anything - "except take exercise, get up early, or be a useful member of the community." But his conversation lacks any ethical responsibility. He lives for nothing except his own pleasure. The beauty of life-especially the superficial beauty of fine clothes, good manners, witty conversation-is all that he cares about.

In his relations with women, Lord Illingworth resembles a very bad bart, indeed. Twenty years after his heartless seduction of Gerald's mother, he refers to her callously as one of his small romances. He carries on a half-serious verbal love affair with Mrs. Allonby, and he does not hesitate to force his attentions on Hester.

Lord Illingworth's only weakness is his sudden affection for Gerald, his new-found son. His punishment is that he cannot get this one thing that he really wants.

Mrs. Allonby

She is a lady of great style. She has beauty, wit, and intelligence. But she suggests a society gone bad, without any basic code of conduct to hold on to. She is an enemy of marriage. Though she is herself engaged in a flirtation with Lord Illingworth, she encourages him to make love to Hester, simply to see whether Hester will object. Her dislike of Hester is indicative of her character. A person with high moral standards is a living reproach to her. Also, she resents Hester's youth.

Lady Hunstanton

Most of the characters in the play are guests at Hunstanton Chase. Their hostess is a pleasant lady who admires Mrs. Arbuthnot's virtuous sweetness, and admits freely that Lord Illingworth's witty remarks her completely confused. She suffers from a faulty memory of a unique kind. (See Comment on Act I.)

Lady Stutfield

She agrees with anybody about anything; thus she seems both obliging and brainless.

Lady Caroline Pontefract

She is the vigilant guardian of Sir John, her fourth husband. She watches his comfort, his health, and especially his contacts with other women. If he even sits next to Lady Stutfield or Mrs. Allonby, she summons him to her side instantly. Sir John does not appear to have the slightest freedom from her constant surveillance.

AN IDEAL HUSBAND

ACT I

SUMMARY

The scene is the home of Sir Robert Chiltern, in London. There is a large party in progress. A chandelier hangs over the staircase by which guests ascend, lighting a French tapestry depicting the "Triumph of Love". On one side is the entrance to the music room. On the other side the entrance leads to other reception rooms.

The scene begins with conversation between two of the guests, Mrs. Marchmont and Lady Basildon. They are very pretty, languid, and clever, but of no particular importance to the play.

Lord Caversham, a gruff but kindly old gentleman, enters and inquires for his son, Lord Goring. He calls him idle and good for nothing. The absent Lord Goring is spiritedly defended by Mabel Chiltern, the young sister of Sir Robert. Mabel is described as exquisitely lovely, like a Tanagra figurine. (Note: Tanagra was a town in Greece where, in the fifth century B.C., beautiful little terra-cotta statuettes were produced.)

Lady Markby now enters with Mrs. Cheveley. Lady Markby is one of Wilde's nice, addle-pated ladies whose conversation is full of strange logic and inspired nonsense. Mrs. Cheveley is tall, red-headed, and distinctly unusual in appearance. She is dressed in heliotrope (lavender) and wears diamonds. Lady Chiltern steps forward to greet her warmly, but she suddenly recognizes Mrs. Cheveley as someone she has known and disliked. She becomes cool in manner.

Sir Robert Chiltern, a handsome, distinguished politician, enters and is introduced to Mrs. Cheveley. She indicates that she has come from Vienna specifically to meet him and to ask a favor from him. She mentions a certain Baron Arnheim, a man now dead whom they both knew. Sir Robert is made uncomfortable by this reference.

This conversation is interrupted by Lord Goring, a young aristocrat whose fashionable exterior conceals a sharp intelligence. He and Mrs. Cheveley know one another. Sir Robert takes Mrs. Cheveley for a tour of his house and its fine paintings. Lord Goring and Mabel Chiltern now have an elaborate flirtatious conversation. It is interrupted when the Vicomte de Nanjac, a young diplomat, offers to escort Mabel to the music room. Mabel has to consent or else appear rude. She is quite annoyed when Lord Goring does not try to stop her. But Lord Goring stays behind to talk to his father, who orders him to keep earlier hours and stop wasting his time at parties. Lord Goring is perfectly polite to his father, but he expertly avoids paying any attention to his advice. When

Mabel returns, he takes her to another room where supper is being served.

After all the guests have gone in to supper, Sir Robert returns with Mrs. Cheveley. That lady proceeds to get down to business. She has invested heavily in an enterprise called the Argentine Canal Company. Sir Robert knows about the scheme. He calls it a swindle. In fact, he is about to submit to Parliament a report which is highly unfavorable to the company. Mrs. Cheveley coolly orders him to suppress this report and make some generally favorable remarks about the company. If he does not, she will publish a letter she has. This letter was written by Sir Robert when he was a young man. In it, he advised Baron Arnheim to buy Suez Canal shares three days before the British government announced its own investment in the shares. In other words, Sir Robert began his rise in the world by selling a government secret when he was a secretary to a Cabinet minister. Sir Robert is thunderstruck. Though he protests and struggles, he is, at last, forced to agree to Mrs. Cheveley's demands.

Comment

Wilde makes use here of a plot full of intrigue, similar to the plots originated by Scribe and imitated by numerous other popular playwrights. (See Introduction.) We find various familiar ingredients of such plays-a fateful letter, a career in danger, a blackmailing adventuress. We must note once more that Wilde handles this material with remarkable skill. The movement of his first act is rapid and varied. He shows dexterity in handling the minor characters who present a bustling, lively scene. His presentation of the involved main situation is clear and polished. When we summarize what he has done, the result may cause our heads to spin. (Mrs. Cheveley, who has known Lady Chiltern in her girlhood, is now trying to blackmail Sir Robert Chiltern. Mrs. Cheveley is also known to Lord Goring, a friend of Sir Robert who is attracted to Mabel, Sir Robert's sister. Etc.) But when we read or see the play itself, all these relationships emerge with effortless clarity.

The characterizations too are fairly successful, though they are revealed only superficially, like all of Wilde's portraits. Mrs. Cheveley, the handsome, exquisite, but sinister lady from Vienna, is quite similar in type to Mrs. Erlynne in *Lady Windermere's Fan*, one of Wilde's best portraits. Wilde is expert at sketching ladies who combine worldly charm with ruthless determination to get what they want, and who are cleverer than their opponents.

Like Mrs. Erlynne, Mrs. Cheveley is an amusing talker. She mentions to Sir Robert that she remembers how his wife used to get good conduct prizes in school. When he asks her what prizes she got, she answers: "My prizes came a little later on in life. I don't think any of them were for good conduct."

Mrs. Cheveley suggests that Sir Robert say a few words in favor of the Argentine Canal Company. She suggests the usual platitudes (common-place, preaching remarks), for there is nothing so effective as a good platitude. "It makes the whole world kin." This is a clever variation of Shakespeare's famous line: "One touch of nature makes the whole world kin." (Troilus and Cressida, Act III, Scene 3.)

Another characterization which Wilde employs effectively is that of Mabel Chiltern. Hers is what is called the ingenue part. That is, she is the young and innocent girl whose obvious destiny is to get married (or at least engaged) before the end of the play. Tastes in such things change, and we may find Mabel more coy and artificial than the young heroines of our own day. But she is a gay contrast to Mrs. Cheveley and she adds vivacity to any scene she appears in.

SUMMARY

While Sir Robert Chiltern is outside getting Mrs. Cheveley's carriage, the other guests and Lady Chiltern return from supper. Mrs. Cheveley tells Lady Chiltern that Sir Robert is going to support the Argentine canal scheme in the House of Commons. (Note: This is the lower house of Parliament, similar to the House of Representatives in the Congress of the United States.) She then leaves, escorted by Sir Robert, while Lady Chiltern, much troubled, rejoins her guests.

Mabel Chiltern and Lord Goring are left alone. Mabel finds a diamond brooch on the sofa. Lord Goring takes it. He asks Mabel not to tell anyone that he has done so. He reveals that he once made someone a present of the brooch some years ago. After the guests have gone, Gertrude Chiltern asks her husband whether Mrs. Cheveley's boast is true. Is he going to support the canal plan? Sir Robert answers that he is going to support it. First he says that he has changed his mind about it; then he admits that he is doing it out of practical necessity.

Lady Chiltern is horrified. She recalls that at school Mrs. Cheveley was a cheat and a liar who was finally expelled for stealing. It is unthinkable that such a person should influence her husband, a man known for his integrity. Then a shocking idea occurs to her. Can it be that her husband has some terrible secret which forces him to do as Mrs. Cheveley asks? If this is true, she says she cannot love him. She loves him for his uprightness, his greatness of soul. He is an ideal to her. If the ideal is shattered, her love is dead.

Sir Robert cannot, after this, admit that his wife's suspicions are true. He sits down and writes a letter to Mrs. Cheveley, in which he takes back his promise to support the canal scheme. His wife insists on this. The letter is sent to Mrs. Cheveley's hotel.

Comment

It becomes plain, as we study *An Ideal Husband*, that in it Oscar While has used many elements from *Lady Windermere's Fan*. This is natural, since it was a great success on the London stage and a better play than *A Woman of No Importance*, which followed. So in this third popular play Wilde once more employed the plot with numerous twists and turns. At the end of Act I, Sir Robert Chiltern is in an intolerable position, caught between two bad alternatives, just as Lord Windermere was. Sir Robert can either knuckle under the blackmailing tactics of Mrs. Cheveley or he can defy her and let her publicize his youthful mistake. In either case, he will lose his wife's love. Lord Windermere had to submit to Mrs. Erlynne's blackmail or have his wife find out about her dishonored mother. He too was in danger of losing his wife's love.

Lady Windermere and Lady Chiltern also have certain similarities. They are both lovely, virtuous, idealistic, and so entirely rigid in their moral standards that they make life difficult for those around them.

The large, glittering social gathering, where many important events of this play take place, is used effectively in both dramas.

Here the minor characters have an excuse for making brief, amusing appearances and lightening the tone of the play with their remarks, frivolous or absurd. For instance, Lady Markby has a theory that intellectual pressure (the necessity of thinking) is bad for debutantes: "It makes the noses of the young girls so particularly large. And there is nothing so difficult to marry as a large nose, men don't like them."

At the very end of Act I, Wilde makes use of symbolism. Sir Robert is alone and desperate. A servant starts to put out the lights. Sir Robert cries: "Put out the lights, Mason, put out the lights." We get the impression that for Sir Robert the lights are going out, and the growing darkness in his house mirrors the darkness in his soul.

At the end of the act, only the great chandelier is still lit. It throws light on the tapestry of the "Triumph of Love". Again the symbol is appropriate. Love has triumphed. It was love for his wife that made Sir Robert write his refusal to Mrs. Cheveley, which will ruin his brilliant career.

ACT II

SUMMARY

It is the next day, in the morning-room of the Chiltern house. Lord Goring and Sir Robert are present. It is clear from their talk that Sir Robert has confided his entire story to Lord Goring and asked for his help. Lord Goring urges Sir Robert to confide in his wife, but he cannot face that prospect. Lord Robert recalls how Baron Arnheim made him understand the glamour of wealth and power. He tells Goring that he got

110,000 pounds from the Baron for the secret information he gave him-enough to start him on his career. (This sum is well over half a million dollars, with much more purchasing power than it would have today.)

Lord Goring promises to help, though he cannot think of anything at present. He reveals incidentally that he was once engaged to Mrs. Cheveley. Sir Robert sends a letter to Vienna inquiring into Mrs. Cheveley's past. He hopes to learn something with which he can counter Mrs. Cheveley's blackmail.

Lady Chiltern enters. Sir Robert goes off to do some work, and she has tea with Lord Goring. They talk about Mrs. Cheveley and the canal scheme. Gently, Lord Goring reproaches Lady Chiltern for her rigid, unforgiving attitude. He points out that anybody can do something foolish or wrong. Charity and love are needed to make life bearable. In sudden pity, he tells Lady Chiltern to come to him for help if she is ever in trouble.

Mabel Chiltern joins them, and the serious moment is over. Before he leaves, Lord Goring asks for a guest list from the previous evening.

Mabel complains to her sister-in-law that Sir Robert's secretary, a young man named Tommy Trafford, is always proposing to her. Then Lady Markby and Mrs. Cheveley come to call. They ask if a diamond brooch has been found; Mrs. Cheveley thinks she may have lost it at the party. Nobody knows anything about it (except Mabel, who has promised not to tell). Lady Markby leaves on another errand, while Mrs. Cheveley stays behind.

As soon as they are alone, Gertrude Chiltern reminds Mrs. Cheveley of her dishonest past and tells her that she wishes no further acquaintance with her. Mrs. Cheveley orders Lady Chiltern to see that Sir Robert keeps his promise about the canal scheme. As Sir Robert himself enters, she tells Lady Chiltern about his sale of a state secret to Baron Arnheim. Sir Robert forces her to leave.

Lady Chiltern expresses her revulsion and horror, now that she knows what her ideal man is really like. Sir Robert responds bitterly that she has made a false idol of him. He wants understanding and love, not worship. Because of her, he has ruined his life. He leaves the room, and Lady Chiltern falls down and sobs on the sofa.

Comment

The most interesting character in Act II is Lord Goring. We see that the conventional man-about-town, the idle dandy, is not empty-headed, as we should expect. He has common sense, sympathy, and a strong sense of right and wrong. He is deeply sorry for Sir Robert, his best friend, but even that will not cause him to hide the truth. What Sir Robert did many years ago was wrong. One way or another, he surely must pay for it. Sir Robert explains that he has been able to build a great political career upon that one bad act. He has been able to use power wisely, to do good for many people. He has given money to charity. But Lord Goring is unconvinced by this defense, though he is willing to help Sir Robert. He also wants to protect Lady Chiltern from the disillusionment which he feels is coming to her.

A great many playwrights make use of characters whose function is to express the views of the playwright himself, to be the voice of common sense. Sometimes this is one of the main characters in the play, like Andrew Undershaft, the millionaire, in Bernard Shaw's *Major Barbara*, or Nora in Henrik Ibsen's *A Doll's House*. Very often it is a secondary character in the play. The family doctor often plays this role. In French drama, this character is called the raisonneur. For Wilde to make a frivolous dandy into a raisonneur is a daring touch of originality.

ACT III

SUMMARY

The scene is Lord Goring's house, which will be the background for a complex game of hide and seek among various characters in the play. Lord Goring, in magnificent evening dress, is in the library. He is about to go out when he reads a note from Lady Chiltern. She needs his help and is coming to see him.

This changes his plans. He tells Phipps, his butler, that he is expecting a lady; Phipps is to show her into the drawing-room. Lord Caversham, Lord Goring's father, chooses this inconvenient moment to visit and lecture his son on the necessity of getting married at once. Lord Caversham complains of a draught, which gives his son an opportunity to move him into the smoking-room.

A lady arrives on schedule, but it is Mrs. Cheveley, not Lady Chiltern. Phipps, who has not been told what lady is coming, directs her to the drawing room, as instructed by his master. Passing the library, Mrs. Cheveley sees and reads lady Chiltern's note. She misunderstands it. It says: "I trust you, I want you. I am coming to you." She assumes it is a love letter. She is about to steal it when Lord Caversham and Lord Goring are heard outside. She retreats into the drawing-room.

Lord Goring shows his father to the door. When he returns, he has Sir Robert with him. Sir Robert has come to get more advice. Lord Goring is uncomfortable. Sir Robert Chiltern is in the library, and he learns from Phipps that the lady he expected is in the drawing-room. Of course, he assumes that the lady is Gertrude Chiltern.

Sir Robert tells Lord Goring that his wife now knows all about what he did. He loves his wife more than anything-far more than his career-but they have quarreled, and he is sure that he has lost her. Lord Goring tells Sir Robert to hope for his wife's forgiveness. If she loves him, she will surely forgive him. Lord Goring hopes that Gertrude Chiltern hears what he is saying.

At this point, a chair is knocked over in the drawing-room. Lord Goring tries to stop him, but Sir Robert rushes in to see who is there. When he comes back to the library he is furious. He calls his friend treacherous and the woman in the drawing-room dishonorable and corrupt. Lord Goring has stayed in the library so he does not know that Mrs. Cheveley is the lady in the drawing-room. He swears that the lady is guiltless and loves Sir Robert. Sir Robert rushes out of the house.

Mrs. Cheveley emerges, obviously enjoying herself. She offers to return Sir Robert's letter if Lord Goring will marry her and assure her of a place in good society. He refuses. But he returns the brooch she lost at the Chilterns'. He transforms it into a bracelet by pressing a secret spring and puts it on her. He then reveals that he gave it to a cousin of his when she got married. Mrs. Cheveley stole it from the cousin's house. Mrs. Cheveley now wishes to deny ever seeing the jewel, but she does not know how to remove it from her arm. Lord Goring threatens to call the police unless she gives him Sir Robert's letter to Baron Arnheim. She does so and he burns it. But before she leaves she steals Lady Chiltern's note. She will send it to Sir Robert. She cannot gain anything by this, but it will satisfy her long hatred of Gertrude Chiltern.

Comment

The action of Act III is exceedingly complex, in the best tradition of popular French plays. Lord Goring adroitly manages to juggle three unwanted guests in three different rooms; he keeps any two of them from meeting until the end of the act. There is something inherently comical in this technique; it reminds us of farces in which philandering wives and jealous husbands are kept separate from one another. In modern times, the Marx brothers used the technique with excellent effect in some of their wilder comic films. However, Wilde's play has comic overtones, and the scene fits into the rest of the play with fair success. In a moving tragedy, this chasing about would be out of place, but in a serio-comic melodrama it is not too disturbing.

The intrigue in this act becomes as involved as the action. To the one letter that is already complicating the Chilterns' lives, a second letter is now added. With these two letters, and with the diamond bracelet-brooch, Lord Goring and Mrs. Cheveley play out an elaborate game. It may be likened to a game of cards or to a fencing duel; the antagonists are cool and expert. Mrs.

Cheveley tries to force Lord Goring into marriage with her by means of the first letter. Lord Goring outsmarts her by means of the diamonds. But she wins the final move by her unscrupulous theft of Lady Chiltern's ambiguously worded pink note.

Meanwhile, Sir Robert adds an extra element to this complex situation. There is an ingenious dialogue between Sir Robert and Lord Goring. Sir Robert is talking about Mrs. Cheveley, but Lord Goring thinks he is referring to Lady Chiltern. At the same time, Lord Goring is taking about Lady Chiltern, but Sir Robert thinks he is referring to Mrs. Cheveley. This device is known as a quid pro quo. It can be found in ancient comedy and also in Abbott and Costello movies. It too is unsuitable to tragedy, but a rather ingenious addition to a melodrama which features a great deal of plot.

Mrs. Cheveley's resemblance to Mrs. Erlynne is strengthened in Act III. Like Mrs. Erlynne, she wishes to get into good society by means of marriage, after she finds that money is not quite enough. However, we must note that, unlike Mrs. Erlynne, Mrs. Cheveley certainly does not have a heart of gold.

A Note: "Lamia-like." When Mrs. Cheveley comes to call on Lord Goring, Wilde describes her green and silver costume as "Lamia-like." A Lamia, according to an old superstition going back to ancient Greece, is a beautiful woman whose real shape is that of a serpent. Keats wrote a striking poem on the subject entitled "Lamia." Wilde is no doubt referring to Mrs. Cheveley's sinister attractiveness. Green and silver are often found in real serpents.

BRIGHT NOTES STUDY GUIDE

ACT IV

SUMMARY

It is the next day. The scene is the morningroom of the Chilterns' home. Here Lord Goring is waiting alone. Sir Robert Chiltern is still at the Foreign Office and Gertrude Chiltern has not come down from her room. Lord Goring is joined by his father, who has been waiting for Sir Robert in another room. He is still full of peppery reproaches for Lord Goring about his idleness and unmarried state. Lord Caversham also tells his son that Sir Robert has made a brilliant speech in the House of Commons condemning the Argentine Canal Company. This is a courageous act, for Sir Robert does not know that Mrs. Cheveley has lost her hold over him.

Mabel Chiltern enters and Lord Caversham leaves. Lord Goring asks her to marry him. She accepts enthusiastically. Gertrude Chiltern now comes in. Mabel goes to wait for Lord Goring in the conservatory. (This is a section of the house where trees and plants are grown.)

Lord Goring gives Lady Chiltern the good news that her husband is safe - the dangerous letter has been burned. But he also tells her that Mrs. Cheveley has stolen her note, which Mrs. Cheveley interprets as a loveletter, and plans to send it to Sir Robert. It is Lord Goring's advice that Lady Chiltern should tell her husband the whole truth. But she cannot face this. She determines to intercept the letter with the help of her husband's secretary.

Just then, Sir Robert rushes in. He has received the note-but since it is not addressed specifically to anyone, he assumes that his wife has written it to him. He is full of joy at being reconciled to her. Lord Goring slips out to the conservatory to join Mabel, after mutely urging Lady Chiltern to accept the situation. She does. She also tells her husband that his letter to Baron Arnheim has been destroyed. He is relieved. However, he feels it is only proper for him to retire from public life, and she eagerly agrees.

Now Lord Goring comes in from the conservatory. Lord Caversham returns too, to tell Sir Robert that he is to have a seat in the Cabinet. Sir Robert refuses it, to Lord Caversham's disgust. Sir Robert goes to write a letter of refusal to the Prime Minister. Lord Goring sends his father into the conservatory to talk with Mabel. Then, alone with Lady Chiltern, he tries to show her what a mistake she is making. If she cuts off her husband from his political career, she will ruin his life. Robbed of his greatness, he will become embittered and eventually cease to love her. Lord Goring says that a woman's role is to forgive her husband, not to judge him. A woman's function in life is to love her husband. Let her not try to do more.

Lady Chiltern is so moved by this speech that, when Sir Robert returns with his letter for the Prime Minister, she tears it up.

Lord Goring now asks Sir Robert's consent for his marriage to his sister. Grateful as he is to Lord Goring, Sir Robert sadly refuses. Remembering that he saw Mrs. Cheveley in Lord Goring's house the night before, he cannot believe that Lord Goring loves only Mabel. Lady Chiltern tells her husband the whole truth - that Lord Goring did not expect Mrs. Cheveley; he expected her, for she intended to come and ask his advice. She also tells him the truth about the note from her - that it was really for Lord Goring. But now she addresses it to her husband and gives it to him. Sir Robert gives his consent to the marriage.

Lord Caversham returns with Mabel. He is delighted to hear that she is to marry his son, and that Sir Robert will accept the Cabinet post after all. Lord Caversham orders Lord Goring to be an ideal husband. Mabel objects to this. He is to be what he likes. She will try to be a real wife.

Comment

This final act is used to unravel all the confusion which has been cunningly created in the earlier acts. It is now the turn of the second letter to be disposed of, the first having been burned up in Act III. Lady Chiltern's note serves here as an instrument of reconciliation between her and her husband. Then it becomes the means for making her see that she must tell her husband the truth, and trust that he will believe her explanation of her note and her visit to Lord Goring. Also, it is used to pave the way for the marriage of Mabel and Lord Goring.

All ends on a note of reconciliation, with the married couple happier than ever, the other engaged, and the quick-tempered Lord Caversham happy for once.

The play is, like Wilde's two previous efforts of this type, thoroughly artificial and contrived, though it is done in a brisk, workmanlike way. It is not quite so impressive as *Lady Windermere's Fan*, since it is a variation on that lively play, and telling a story for a second time seldom improves it. But it is free of the sticky sentimentality and absurd oratory of *A Woman of No Importance.*

As in the two earlier plays, Wilde gives the impression that he has a message to deliver. This message concerns the nature of marriage. A reexamination of the institution of marriage was in the air in the 1890s. It was stimulated by the new interest in the education and citizenship of women. Her place in the marital relationship was being evaluated in the light of these new ideas. We find this subject discussed in the explosive "new drama" of the era - that of Ibsen, Strindberg, and George Bernard Shaw. These evoked a number of pale imitations in the work of Pinero, Jones, and Wilde himself.

Ibsen's views on marriage were revolutionary: he visualized the woman as an individual entity whose first duty was to herself. (See *A Doll's House*). Strindberg reacted against this view: he foresaw terrible consequences if women rejected their female natures. (See *Miss Julie*.) Bernard Shaw tended to sympathize with the revolutionary viewpoint, but he added his own unique wit and insight to the discussion. (See especially *Man and Superman*.)

Wilde too discusses this very fashionable subject. His message is that women should not idealize their husbands, nor try to direct their lives. He presents this idea with a flourish, but even in the 1890s it was not startling. As a thinker about human problems, Wilde is undistinguished. As a comic writer he has authentic greatness. At the time of this play, the greatness is still a promise (in Lord Caversham, Mrs. Cheveley, Lord Goring). Its fruition is soon to come.

BRIGHT NOTES STUDY GUIDE

CHARACTERIZATIONS

Mrs. Cheveley

She is a successful example of a type that Wilde portrays very well - the goodlooking, intelligent, amusing, unscrupulous adventuress. She is thus a relative of Mrs. Erlynne in *Lady Windermere's Fan* and Mrs. Allonby in *A Woman of No Importance*. She is deceptively languid and very dangerous. She has no redeeming traits of character.

Sir Robert Chiltern

Sir Robert is a proud, distinguished man who freely admits that he enjoys wealth and political power. He is devoted to his wife and fond of his friend, Lord Goring. But outside of them, he seems to have few deep personal relations.

In the course of the play, Sir Robert reaches new understanding. He finds that it is impossible to excuse his early dishonest action because he used it for good ends. He faces up to the fact that what he did was wrong. His moral courage is also shown by his speech against the Argentine Canal scheme, for he believes that he will be ruined by Mrs. Cheveley for speaking out against it. In general, Sir Robert, by the end of the play, actually becomes as morally splendid as everyone says he is at the beginning. He grows into a man who matches his reputation.

Lady Gertrude Chiltern

An idealistic woman who loves her husband for his noble nature. Lady Chiltern is a good person who is unfortunately rigid in her code of values - "pitiless in her perfection," as her sorely tried but admiring husband describes her. She learns that one cannot give love as a reward for virtue-one must give it freely, without conditions. She learns that a woman who loves should be able to forgive. She is generally similar to Lady Windermere in *Lady Windermere's Fan*.

Lord Goring

Lord Goring is a man-about-town who gives the impression of talking nonsense and thinking only about his dress. But this facade conceals a man of deep sympathy and human wisdom who is able to help both his friend and his friend's wife. He is the voice of good sense, the raisonneur, in the play.

Mabel Chiltern

She is the play's ingenue - the pretty young romantic lead. After the fashion of 1895, she is a pert, affected young thing who is amply aware of her own charm. But though she may not be entirely to the modern taste, she is a gay, vivacious element in the play.

Lord Caversham

This gruff old gentleman is perpetually irritated with his son. He finds him lazy and useless; he has not even gotten married. There is **irony** in this, since this irate parent misunderstands his son completely and seems to know nothing of his true nature.

Though Lord Caversham cannot **refrain** from barking fiercely at almost everybody, he is good-hearted. He is pleased at Sir Robert's success. He is obviously fond of his son, and he is quite susceptible to pretty women.

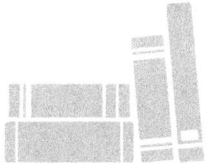

THE IMPORTANCE OF BEING EARNEST

ACT I

SUMMARY

The scene is Algernon Moncrieff's flat (apartment) in Half-Moon Street, London. Algernon's perfect servant, Lane, is setting out afternoon tea. The sound of a piano can be heard from another room. When the music stops, Algernon enters the room.

Algernon asks Lane whether he has made cucumber sandwiches for his aunt, Lady Bracknell. Lane produces the platter of sandwiches, and Algernon takes two. He continues to eat cucumber sandwiches as the scene progresses. Lane announces that Mr. Ernest Worthing is calling. Ernest enters; in response to Algernon's questions, he says that he has been in the country for the past few days. Casually, Algernon mentions the fact that Ernest's country place is in the county of Shropshire. Ernest agrees that this is correct.

Ernest comments on the elaborate tea preparations. Algernon tells him that his Aunt Augusta (Lady Bracknell) and his cousin Gwendolen are coming to tea. Ernest is delighted to hear this, for he is clearly much attracted to Gwendolen. But Algernon does not think his aunt will approve of Ernest's presence; Ernest is not a desirable suitor for her daughter. Ernest tells Algernon that he has come to London just to propose to Gwendolen.

He is about to take a cucumber sandwich when Algernon restrains him. The cucumber sandwiches are reserved for Aunt Augusta. Indignantly, Ernest points out that Algernon has been eating them the whole time. Algernon points out, with questionable logic, that she is his aunt. He urges bread and butter on Ernest; the bread and butter is meant for Gwendolen.

Algernon now shows Ernest a cigarette case he left in the flat on a previous visit. Algernon points out that there is an inscription engraved on the case which is signed: "Cecily." Who, Algernon asks, is Cecily? Reluctantly, Ernest replies that Cecily is his aunt. Why then, Algernon inquires, does she sign herself: "From little Cecily with her fondest love?" Ernest impatiently answers that she happens to be a small aunt. Adroitly holding the cigarette case out of Ernest's reach, Algernon asks why his aunt Cecily addresses the inscription to "her dear Uncle Jack."

Ernest is forced to explain fully. In the first place, his name is really Jack, not Ernest. In his country home lives his ward, Cecily Cardew, a very pretty girl eighteen years of age. As the legal guardian of Cecily, he must behave in a grave, highly respectable manner. In order to get an occasional rest from this high moral tone, Jack has invented a younger brother, Ernest, who lives in London and is constantly getting into trouble. At intervals, Jack comes up to London to rescue Ernest from another one of his scrapes.

Algernon asks for Jack's country address, but Jack will not give it to him. He says triumphantly that it is not in Shropshire. Jack plans to keep Algernon away from Cecily; Cecily is a rather susceptible young girl. She has shown some romantic interest in the wicked (though imaginary) Ernest.

Algy says that Jack is a "Bunburyist." Jack has invented a younger brother Ernest in order that he may get out of the country and enjoy himself in London. Algy himself has invented an invalid friend named Bunbury who lives in the country, in order that he may leave London (and his relatives) and enjoy himself in the country whenever he wishes.

Jack expresses his intention of killing off Ernest if he should succeed in getting engaged to Gwendolen. Algy protests that a man needs a Bunbury more than ever when he is married. Algy offers to get his aunt out of the way so that Jack can propose to Gwendolen-if Jack will buy him dinner. He plans to get out of dining at his Aunt Augusta's house with the help of Bunbury.

Comment

In this play, Wilde has made a strong and brilliant development as a dramatist. At one stroke, he has eliminated the second-hand melodrama which was the mainstay of the earlier plays. The good women and adventuresses are gone. So are the moral dilemmas and the lessons in human relations. Those elements of the other plays which remain, such as intrigue, the ancient secret, the tangled romances, have altered drastically.

For example, in the scene described above, we have the party scene which is featured in *Lady Windermere's Fan* and

An Ideal Husband. But it has changed; the concert in the music room has become Algernon's offstage piano solo, played "with wonderful expression," though not accurately. The glittering assemblage has shrunk to one guest, who is soon augmented by two more. The scene has become smaller, less pretentious, with a new range of possibilities.

In this first act, the main purpose is what we call "**exposition**" - the explanation of who is who and what situation they find themselves in. As in the other plays, Wilde has some very complicated explanations to make which he manages with clarity and skill. Here, the situation is not only complex but totally absurd-it comprises Jack's imaginary friend Bunbury, the susceptible Cecily, the flirtatious Gwendolen, and the looming figure of Lady Bracknell. We have been transported to a world where there is much to-do about very little.

Further evidence that we are in a peculiar new world is afforded by the upside-down nature of the conversation. Lane confides to Algernon that he does not know much about marriage: he has only been married once. He does not think about it much for it is an uninteresting subject. Algernon comments that if the lower classes do not set a good moral example, what is the use of them? The discussion is preposterous but vaguely familiar. We soon realize that we have heard such remarks before, only we have heard them the other way around. It is the upper classes whose duty it is supposed to be to set a good moral example to the lower classes.

In another place, Jack tells Algernon that once he is married he will certainly not want anything to do with Bunbury. Algernon replies: "Then your wife will." He adds that in marriage, three is company and two is none. Again the expression is familiar, but it is upside down. Normally, two is company and three is none (or three is a crowd, as we would say). By turning it around, the author throws a new light on the subject.

SUMMARY

Lady Bracknell and Gwendolen arrive. Lady Bracknell greets her nephew but bestows only a very aloof bow on Jack. Gwendolen, however, sits down in a corner with Jack. She refuses courteously but firmly to move over next to her mother.

Lady Bracknell requests the cucumber sandwiches Algernon has promised her. Algernon goes to the table and finds only the empty plate - the natural result of his having eaten all the sandwiches. He expresses shock and distress. He asks Lane why there are no cucumber sandwiches. That invaluable servant replies that there were no cucumbers to be had in the market - "not even for ready money." (This conjures up a wild image of Lane buying cucumbers on margin, like securities, or perhaps with the aid of a bank loan.)

Algernon reveals that he will not be able to dine with his aunt; Bunbury has taken a turn for the worse. Lady Bracknell, in an exasperated tone, wishes that Bunbury would make up his mind whether he is going to live or die.

Algernon takes Lady Bracknell into another room to discuss the music that will be played at a reception she is planning. Left alone with Gwendolen, Jack makes a cautious conversational opening; he talks about the weather. Gwendolen is made impatient by this. She encourages him to speak up before her mother returns. Before he has gotten fairly started, she admits her love for him-especially because his name is Ernest.

Jack is overjoyed at her confession of love. But he is a bit disquieted to think that she loves him because his name is Ernest. After all, his name is not Ernest. He suggests that Jack is a nice name. Gwendolen disapproves of the name Jack.

Jack begins to talk of marriage. But Gwendolen insists on being proposed to in a proper ceremonial manner. Jack gets down on one knee and does so. This is the moment when Lady Bracknell returns to the room.

Gwendolen tells her mother that she and Jack (or Ernest, as she calls him) are engaged. Her mother replies that she will tell Gwendolen when she is engaged. She sends Gwendolen out to the carriage, to wait while she questions Jack.

Jack's answers to Lady Bracknell's questions are satisfactory, as regards age, occupation, and income. But a question about his parentage reveals that he was a foundling. A Mr. Thomas Cardew found him as an infant in a large black handbag, in a cloakroom at Victoria Station. Lady Bracknell tells Jack that unless he can produce proper relatives, he can have no hope of marrying Gwendolen. She leaves indignantly.

Gwendolen comes back. She fears her mother will never permit her to marry Jack. She takes down his address in the country so that she can communicate with him daily. With great satisfaction at the opportunity, Algernon also takes down the country address where Cecily, eighteen and very pretty, is living.

Comment

The scene in which Lady Bracknell looks into the credentials of her future son-in-law is one of the most famous and amusing in English literature. It is a superb blend of nonsense and light satire.

One element which makes the scene amusing is the upside-down conversation, characteristic of the entire play. (We usually call a statement which is opposite to what we might expect, a paradox.) Those answers which we would expect Lady Bracknell to object to, she finds pleasing. Jack admits that he smokes. She is glad to hear it, because a man should have some occupation. Jack also admits that he knows nothing. She approves. Nothing should tamper with the "delicate exotic fruit" - ignorance - or it loses its bloom.

The scene is also a fine bit of **satire**. It is ironical to observe that when Wilde strikes the pose of a social critic, as he does in the three earlier plays we have dealt with, he achieves a result that is both strained and banal. But when he abandons himself to the bubbling gaiety that is his true excellence, he achieves highly effective social criticism with an appearance of perfect ease.

Lady Bracknell is a caricature of all the tough-minded mothers who have ever gone about the task of finding the proper husbands for their daughters. The proper husband, of course, has certain criteria to meet-social, professional, financial. In real life, these matters are often looked into discreetly. But Lady Bracknell offers no pretenses; she is entirely open about this. She begins by efficiently producing a pad and pencil, with which she makes notes during the interview. She tells Jack that he is not on her list of eligible young men - and she uses the same list as the Duchess of Bolton.

The eminent practicality of Lady Bracknell's behavior is very funny. It is as though Jack were either a piece of livestock or a financial investment she were considering. But behind the absurdity there is sharp criticism of the way, in certain classes of society, marriages are arranged for financial and social reasons, with little interest in whether the parties to the marriage care for each other. Alfred Lord Tennyson discusses this subject seriously in his narrative poem "Maud" (1855). William Makepeace Thackeray gives it extended satirical treatment in his great novel, *Vanity Fair* (1848). From these examples (many more could be given), we see that this subject was of great interest to the nineteenth century. No treatment of it is sharper or surer than Wilde's, however.

We may also note that the Duchess of Berwick, in *Lady Windermere's Fan*, is a character of the same type as Lady Bracknell, but less fully developed. Obedient Agatha, however, is very different from Gwendolen, who is high-spirited and independent.

ACT II

SUMMARY

The scene is the Manor House at Woolton, where Cecily Cardew, Jack Worthing's ward, lives with her governess, Miss Prism. In the garden, Cecily is trying to delay her German lesson. She dislikes all her subjects, but German the most. She waters the flowers, talks with Miss Prism about the wicked young man, Jack's younger brother Ernest, and then writes in her diary. Miss Prism reveals during their talk that she once wrote a three-volume novel.

> Canon Chasuble, the local clergyman, now enters. Cecily arranges for Miss Prism to take a walk with him. Miss Prism seems to find the Canon a romantic figure, though he is elderly and very scholarly in his conversation.

Comment

Wilde shows skill in the names he gives to some of his characters. They suggest the kind of people he is portraying; sometimes they are small caricatures all by themselves. When one says the name "Miss Prism," for instance, one cannot help pursing one's lips in a prim manner, which suggests the ultra-respectable, schoolteacherish lady who bears the name.

Canon Chasuble's name suggests the dignified, conservative churchman. A canon is a clergyman attached to a cathedral church - that is, a church which houses a bishop. A chasuble is a vestment worn during celebration of the mass by priests-either Catholic or conservative Anglican priests who practice a ritual very similar to that of the Catholics.

Dr. Chasuble's learning is deeper than Miss Prism's. He refers to her as "Egeria," which bewilders her. Egeria is the name of a nymph in Latin mythology; her main characteristic was her wisdom. The nymph frequently gave advice to Numa Pompilius, an early Roman king-so says legend.

However, Miss Prism does have a realistic attitude toward life. When discussing her novel, she says that in it, the good ended happily, and the bad people did not. "That is what Fiction means." In other words, such exact justice is seldom found in real life.

She is also quite unsentimental about the wicked Ernest. She does not believe in reforming him-in "turning bad people into good people at a moment's notice." If he is bad, she thinks he should be punished, and let that be the end of it.

SUMMARY

> While Cecily is alone with her books, Mr. Ernest Worthing is announced. Cecily is much pleased; the wicked Ernest has at last arrived in person. The butler brings Algernon into the garden. He assures Cecily that he is not wicked at all. This disappoints her so obviously that he admits that he has been quite reckless and bad. He urges her to reform him. Since she claims she is too busy, he decides to reform himself during the course of the afternoon. But this will require nourishment; Algernon is hungry, as usual. Cecily takes him into the house for food.

Dr. Chasuble and Miss Prism return; Miss Prism is reproaching him for being a bachelor. She feels he needs a wife-a mature one, of course.

Jack Worthing now enters, dressed in deep mourning. His brother Ernest, he announces, is dead, carried off by a severe chill while in Paris. (Jack has killed off Ernest in preparation for his marriage to Gwendolen, as he planned to in Act I.) For Gwendolen's sake, Jack arranges to have Dr. Chasuble christen him Ernest later in the afternoon.

Cecily comes out of the house. She tells her guardian that his brother Ernest is inside. She then brings Algernon out into the garden. Algernon tells "Brother Jack" that he is sorry for all the wrong he has done. He means to lead a better life from now on. Jack is simply furious with Algernon, but Cecily forces them to shake hands. Dr. Chasuble, Miss Prism, and Cecily leave the garden, so that the reconciled brothers can be alone. When they are alone, Jack learns that Algernon has brought a pile of luggage and has settled in for a week's stay. Jack orders Algernon to return to London at once; he then goes to take off his mourning costume.

Algernon is quite unrepentant, and when the charming Cecily returns, he gives up the idea of leaving. He declares his love. She writes down what he says in her diary. He asks her to marry him. She tells him they have been engaged for the past three months, and shows him his letters to her, which she has had to write herself. Algernon is bewildered but joyful to find that his romance with Cecily has been going on for months. The only thing that is disturbing is her statement that she could only love a man named Ernest. Hastily, Algernon goes off to arrange his christening by Dr. Chasuble.

Comment

We are not too surprised to find that in her cautious romance with Dr. Chasuble, Miss Prism takes the active role. That bumbling gentleman can only back away clumsily from her attack. She accuses him of being a "woman-thrope," a hater of women, a word she has invented as a companion to "misanthrope," a hater of man. (It actually refers to the whole human race, not the male sex.) Dr. Chasuble takes refuge in the church, where, he says, early practice did not include marriage for the clergy.

It is more startling to observe the successful tactics of Cecily. She is young and naive. Yet she takes the lead in Algernon's courtship with complete self-confidence. She does quite as well as the sophisticated Gwendolen did in the first act. With the help of wide-eyed innocence ("I do not think it can be right for you to talk to me like that. Miss Prism never says such things to me," she remarks to Algernon when he tells her she is like a pink rose) and her diary, she becomes affianced to Algernon in record time.

Cecily's diary is the occasion of a light satirical touch. Cecily remarks that it is only a record of a young girl's thoughts and "consequently meant for publication." This refers to the great numbers of journals and diaries which were published with the claim that when they were written, they were not meant for publication-a claim which is very hard to believe. In our day, many such books are still printed, and we still suspect that the authors always meant to publish them.

SUMMARY

Cecily is alone once more in the garden when Gwendolen Fairfax is announced by the butler. Gwendolen is effusively friendly. They are soon on a first-name basis. She is taken aback to learn that Mr. Worthing is Cecily's guardian. She is not pleased to think that her fiance has a ward so young and pretty. She is soon reassured. Cecily is the ward of John Worthing, not Ernest Worthing. In fact, Cecily confides, she is engaged to Ernest Worthing. On the contrary, Gwendolen remarks courteously, she is engaged to Ernest Worthing. Courtesy disappears. At the height of a sharp verbal duel between the girls, Jack returns.

Gwendolen greets Jack lovingly as Ernest. Cecily tells her that this is Mr. Jack Worthing, her guardian. Gwendolen draws away from Jack at the terrible news that his name is not Ernest.

Next Algernon returns, and the same things happen. Cecily greets him as Ernest, Gwendolen reveals his real name, and Cecily recoils from him in horror.

Now Gwendolen and Cecily are drawn together. They are fellow-victims of a cruel deception. With arms about one another's waist, they go together into the house. Jack and Algernon are left outside at the teatable. Jack is in a severely agitated state, but Algernon is enjoying his latest **episode** of Bunburying. He systematically devours all the muffins at the tea table, as the act comes to an end.

Comment

When its basic elements are examined, the structure of *The Importance of Being Earnest* is like that of Wilde's earlier plays. The first act is employed to introduce the characters and explain their relation to one another. This is known as the **exposition**. In the first act, the main action is also begun. (Jack, Algernon, and Gwendolen are all started on their way to the Manor House.)

The second act is the one in which complications are introduced and affairs reach a **climax**. In the third act, all elements are sorted out and concluded. Act II provides a full measure of events which follow one another rapidly and create even more complications. The pace becomes faster as the act proceeds. Algernon's arrival as Ernest is quickly followed by Jack's arrival in mourning for Ernest, dead in Paris of a chill. Soon after, Algernon and Cecily confess their love and agree to marry. Then comes the arrival of Gwendolen and first the quarrel, then the reconciliation of the two girls.

The only way in which all this frantic action differs from what we find in *An Ideal Husband* or the other plays is that it is about nothing whatever. Nobody's career or happiness is seriously at stake. The excitement is entirely because two couples have gotten engaged with the girl in each case believing that her young man's name is Ernest, and the girls have now found out that their fiances are not named Ernest at all. The absurdity of the problem is only equalled by its unlikelihood. How delightful to spend a couple of hours in a world of gaiety and wit, where young lovers are divided only by problems as insubstantial as smoke!

The encounter between Cecily and Gwendolen is one of the most subtly written sections of the play. Immediately after they meet, we feel between them the antagonism of two pretty women who come together without preparation or warning, and who cannot identify one another clearly. This is made worse because Cecily knows this beautiful lady has something to do with her guardian, and Gwendolen has the disagreeable experience of finding this pretty girl living in the home of her fiance.

Gwendolen handles her obvious dislike by expressing its opposite. She insists that she likes Cecily the moment she sees her. Cecily, on the other hand, is more reserved. She lets Gwendolen pour forth exaggerated sentiments, but she responds with conventional politeness, no more. This throws Gwendolen slightly off balance and puts her at a disadvantage.

When the girls believe they are both engaged to the same man and become openly hostile, we are amused to see how the battle goes. The underdog is Cecily. She is only eighteen. She has grown up in the country, and has been under the control of the dubiously intelligent Miss Prism for three years. Gwendolen is older, and she is the product of sophisticated London society. Yet Cecily emerges as the victor in the verbal battle. Almost every thrust of Gwendolen's is topped by a successful retort by Cecily.

For example, when it becomes apparent that Gwendolen was engaged to Ernest Worthing before Cecily, Gwendolen says she has the prior claim. Cecily replies that Ernest seems to have changed his mind since his engagement to Gwendolen. Cecily also takes direct action when she gives Gwendolen four lumps of sugar in her tea and a large slice of cake, after Gwendolen has requested no sugar and bread and butter. But her most triumphant stroke is her final comment: "It seems to me, Miss Fairfax, that I am trespassing on your valuable time. No doubt you have many other calls of a similar character to make in the neighborhood."

The reversal of the quarrel is also most amusing. Within a moment, the two wronged girls are full of passionate sympathy for one another. They decide to call one another "sister," thus carrying out Algernon's observation in Act I that women only call each other sister when they have called each other a lot of other things first.

The act ends at a point of thorough confusion. Each set of young lovers has quarrelled. And in the background there is still the threat of Lady Bracknell.

ACT III

SUMMARY

In the morning-room of the Manor House, Gwendolen and Cecily are looking out of the window at Jack and Algy. They are rather disturbed at being ignored by the young men, for they are now ready to receive apologies and be reconciled. They are willing to look upon anything as a sign that the young men are sorry. Cecily notices that they are eating muffins; she accepts this as repentance.

The men enter. The girls agree to be silent; they will not be the first to speak. Accordingly, Gwendolen is the first to speak. She asks for an explanation. Algernon explains that he pretended to be the wicked Ernest in order to meet Cecily. Jack explains that he pretended to have a brother in order to come to London and see Gwendolen. The girls are satisfied with these explanations. They are beautiful, even if not true. As Gwendolen says, "In matters of grave importance, style, not sincerity, is the vital thing." (This might well be the motto of the society Wilde is satirizing.)

The girls, however, are still desirous of marrying men named Ernest. Jack and Algy tell them they are each going to be christened Ernest later in the afternoon. Cecily and Gwendolen are so moved by this self-sacrifice that they forgive the young men. The two pairs of lovers fall into one another's arms, just as Lady Bracknell enters.

Lady Bracknell has followed Gwendolen, after bribing Gwendolen's maid to learn where she has gone. She once more tells Jack that there can be no engagement between him and Gwendolen.

Now she turns to Algernon. What, she asks, has happened to his friend Mr. Bunbury? Bunbury is dead, Algernon replies. Lady Bracknell is glad to hear that Mr. Bunbury has at last done something definite about his illness. She would also like to know whose hand her nephew is holding.

Jack introduces Cecily to Lady Bracknell. Cecily and Algernon tell her they are engaged. Lady Bracknell is disturbed at the high percentage of engagements she has met with recently. However, she sets to work gathering information about Cecily. She begins with an acid inquiry: is Cecily connected with any of the London Railway stations? Jack is very angry at this indirect thrust at him. But he controls himself. He gives full information about his ward. As Lady Bracknell is about to leave, Jack tells her that Cecily has a fortune of one hundred and thirty thousand pounds. Lady Bracknell sits down again abruptly.

She now finds Cecily most attractive, full of the solid good qualities that last. She tells her frankly that Algernon has no money, but Lady Bracknell does not believe in mercenary marriages! She adds that she had no money at all when she married Lord Bracknell but she did not let that stop her.

Jack interrupts this happy scene. He will not give his consent. He suspects Algernon of being untruthful by nature. All are astounded by this charge. It is impossible! Algernon went to Oxford!

But Jack is firm. And since, by the terms of her grandfather's will, Cecily will not come of age until she is thirty-five, his objections are serious. Lady Bracknell does not see anything wrong with waiting until Cecily is thirty-five, but Cecily does not care for this idea at all.

> Jack does point out that if Lady Bracknell will permit Gwendolen to marry him, he will permit Cecily to marry Algernon. This Lady Bracknell refuses to consider. She and Gwendolen prepare to leave.

Comment

At the beginning of Act III, the estrangements between the lovers disappear in a cloud of nonsense. The scene has a comic-opera quality, and is indeed in part a **satire** on popular comedies and operettas. In their discussion, Gwendolen and Cecily tend to speak at the same time-which happens very often in operettas. However, they recognize that this is a difficult thing to accomplish. They talk it over beforehand and Gwendolen conducts them as they speak. This is a genial joke at the expense of plays and operettas where several characters speak the same words in perfect unison, apparently without effort.

Note that in this act, Algernon kills off his imaginary friend Bunbury. This is in contradiction to what he says in Act I - that Bunbury is particularly necessary to a married man. Algernon must be very much in love with Cecily to have changed his mind.

Lady Bracknell's reappearance gives new color and a change of tone to the play. She is a creation so formidable that she carries a strong atmosphere of her own. Her mental processes are not unlike those of the elderly society ladies in Wilde's other plays, except that she is in no way muddleheaded, as are Lady Hunstanton and Lady Markby. Her memory is competent and her intellect strong, though it does operate according to a system of its own. For instance, when she hears of Algernon's engagement, she remarks that the number of engagements hereabouts seems "considerably above the proper average that statistics have laid down for our guidance." This seems sensible until a close examination shows us that it is a prime example of upside-down thinking. Statistics do not guide behavior; they record it. Upon further consideration, we realize that this is one of Wilde's most profound jokes. Many people do behave as though they are supposed to try to conform to statistical averages; they become upset if their wishes and thoughts are not the same as "the average."

This second scene between Jack Worthing and Lady Bracknell is amusing because in part the tables are turned. Jack once more supplies Lady Bracknell with vital information, this time about Cecily instead of about himself. But as soon as Lady Bracknell learns of Cecily's substantial fortune, Jack is in a position of power. Cecily is a most eligible young lady-especially for the penniless Algernon. Lady Bracknell is anxious for the match to take place, even if it means waiting seventeen years, until Cecily is thirty-five. But since Cecily will not wait until then- which, to Lady Bracknell, shows "a somewhat impatient nature" - Jack, as her guardian, controls the situation. He obviously enjoys standing up to Lady Bracknell and telling her she must let him marry Gwendolen before he will permit Cecily to marry Algernon. Otherwise, as he puts it, "a passionate celibacy" is their future destiny.

As Lady Bracknell looks Cecily over, she is critical of her appearance. Her dress is "sadly simple." Her hair looks "almost as Nature might have left it." No doubt, Wilde is referring satirically to society beauties who are so artificial that they no longer bear much resemblance to women in their natural state. Cecily's youth and prettiness are not good enough for Lady Bracknell who wants her completely changed by a good French maid. She tells how she recommended one to a certain lady of her acquaintance, and in three months her own husband did not know her. Jack comments that, after six months, nobody knew her. (That is, she had so disgraced herself by her behavior that she was a social outcast.)

SUMMARY

Dr. Chasuble now enters. He is much disappointed when he is told that there will be no christenings. (Since nobody can get married anyway, the christenings have no practical value.) He says he will return to the church, where Miss Prism is waiting for him.

At the sound of this name, Lady Bracknell is startled. When she learns Miss Prism is Cecily's governess, she demands to see her. At this moment, Miss Prism arrives, looking for Canon Chasuble. She is shocked when she sees Lady Bracknell. Lady Bracknell demands to know where the baby is that was left in Miss Prism's charge twenty-eight years ago. The baby's carriage was found, and in it was the manuscript of a three-volume novel, but the baby was missing.

Miss Prism explains that in a moment of absent-mindedness she put the manuscript of her novel in the carriage and the baby in a black leather handbag. She put the handbag in the cloakroom at Victoria Station.

Jack, much excited, rushes upstairs to get the handbag. Miss Prism identifies it as hers. Jack embraces her and call her "mother," to her great indignation. She is unmarried. Jack tells her it does not matter and tries to embrace her again.

Lady Bracknell tells Jack that Miss Prism is not his mother. He is the child of General and Mrs. Moncrieff and thus is Algernon's older brother. "What is his name, then?" Jack asks. "Why," Lady Bracknell answers, "he was named for his father". She cannot remember the General's Christian name. Jack looks up the General in a military directory and learns that his name was Ernest John Moncrieff. Jack has told Gwendolen the truth after all. His name really is Earnest.

At this news, Canon Chasuble embraces Miss Prism (for no logical reason), Algernon embraces Cecily, and Jack embraces Gwendolen. Jack says that for the first time in his life he realizes *The Importance of Being Earnest*. With this purposely dreadful pun, the play ends.

Comment

Lady Bracknell's description of Miss Prism ("a female of repellent aspect, remotely connected with education") is a famous line from this play. However, it is only part of a very funny dialogue between Lady Bracknell and Canon Chasuble. Canon Chasuble is angry at this description. He says that Miss Prism is a most cultivated and respectable lady. To this, Lady Bracknell replies grimly: "It is obviously the same person." Lady Bracknell has, so to speak, translated the Canon's remark and found that it checks with her own description. If the lady is cultivated, she is no doubt a governess, and if she is very respectable, she is probably very plain in appearance.

When Lady Bracknell confronts Miss Prism, she acts as if no time has elapsed since she saw her last. "Prism! Where is that baby?" cries Lady Bracknell, as if she were taking up an interrupted conversation.

Miss Prism's story of her confused actions twenty-eight years before, which results in Jack learning who he is, is a **satire** on a whole mass of dramatic literature. In this literature, children are mixed up in infancy and only learn who they are when they are grown up, usually at a crucial point in their lives. Plays using this device are found as far back as the work of the Roman Plautus (died 184 B.C.).

This device is still to be found in the plays and operas of the nineteenth century. It is not very likely that Miss Prism would put a baby into a handbag instead of his carriage and then check the handbag at a railway station. But it is not more incredible than what is seriously shown in Verdi's opera *Il Trovatore* (1852): the gypsy woman Azucena, holding both her own baby and the child of her enemy, throws the enemy's child into a fire-only she finds out a moment later that she has incinerated her own child by mistake. Wilde is amiably making fun of this type of nonsense.

William S. Gilbert also satirized it in his libretto for the operetta *H.M.S. Pinafore* (1878); here Little Buttercup describes how she mixed up two babies when she was a nursemaid. One is now a sea captain and one a common sailor. As soon as they learn of the error, they dutifully switch positions and accents; the former cockney sailor now speaks a cultivated English and the former captain talks like a cockney sailor. Gilbert, unlike Wilde, was acutely aware of the absurdities of class distinction. Wilde only notices the absurdities of second-rate plays.

In fact, Wilde has crowded a surprising amount of literary **satire** into the recognition scene of *The Importance of Being Earnest*. Not only do we have the long-lost baby and the absent-minded nursemaid, we also have the illegitimate child and the unmarried mother, whom he recognizes at long last and defends against the world. Among the numerous plays of this kind which Wilde laughs at is *A Woman of No Importance*, by Oscar Wilde. Jack says to Miss Prism (mistakenly): "But after all, who has the right to cast a stone against one who has suffered? Cannot repentance wipe out an act of folly? Why should there be one law for men and another for women? Mother, I forgive you." This could have been taken straight out of Wilde's earlier play. Miss Prism's indignation at this familiar and well-meant speech makes it all the funnier.

The Importance of Being Earnest is one of the great comedies of the English language. In it, Oscar Wilde has created a complete world, entirely light and frivolous. This world is inhabited by unreal people who converse in a manner more witty, more elegant, and more absurd than that of everyday human beings. Their normal method of expression is the paradox, or upside-down statement. ("A girl with a simple, unspoiled nature, like Gwendolen, could hardly be expected to reside in the country.") They also talk sheer nonsense. ("When I am in really great trouble, as anyone who knows me intimately will tell you, I refuse everything except food and drink.") They employ a strange brand of logic. ("I have lost both my parents." "Both? That seems like carelessness.")

Nothing of any real importance happens in the world of this comedy. The events are incredible. They are brought to a conclusion by the most fantastic kind of coincidence.

But any descriptive effort is likely to be a failure with this play. It is a complete and perfect whole; the events, the characters, the dialogue all blend into one another to form an indescribable experience, not the less significant because it is pleasurable and easy to grasp. Those examples of wit and style which are given here are arbitrarily chosen. A completely different assortment, every bit as good, could easily have been assembled. Each reader is amused by the play in a slightly different way. As each person gets to know it, he gathers his own selection of favorite moments and favorite lines.

Oscar Wilde seems to have come to this remarkable work via a gradual development. Similar characters and dialogues are found scattered through his earlier plays, but they are usually subsidiaries of a rather ordinary main plot, and they are not fully developed. Eventually, Wilde tossed away the ordinary people and events and worked only with the gay caricatures and witty nonsense he had previously experimented with. The Duchess of Berwick became Lady Bracknell, and Lord Goring was turned into Gwendolen Fairfax.

There is nothing else in English literature quite like *The Importance of Being Earnest*. However, in the late seventeenth century, there was a group of comic dramatists (often known as Restoration playwrights) who produced comedies which were light, artificial, and polished in style. The greatest of these was William Congreve. His plays, *Love for Love* (1695) and *The Way of the World* (1700) have a gay brilliance of style which is not dissimilar to Wilde's.

CHARACTERIZATIONS

At no time in his career does Oscar Wilde show much talent for profound, believable character portraits. His interest in his fellow men is always superficial rather than analytical. He does not belong with those who reveal to us our fellow human beings and thus increase our understanding and our sympathy. He does not belong with Shakespeare, Chaucer, Browning - nor with Tennessee Williams, Arthur Miller, and similar writers of our own time.

In *The Importance of Being Earnest*, a play which is all polished surface, the character portraits are also concerned only with surfaces. This is to be expected. But in this limited kind of portraiture, Wilde is very skillful at differentiating the characters and giving them distinctive characteristics. The two young men, Jack and Algernon, are clearly distinguishable from one another. There is little danger of confusing Gwendolen with Cecily. Shakespeare himself was not as successful at differentiating the young lovers in his early comedies.

The other roles too, are clearly drawn, though with the clarity of cartoons - the imposing Lady Bracknell, the respectable Miss Prism, and Canon Chasuble, the likeable though boring clergyman.

Jack Worthing

Jack is the older and more serious of the two young men. He is also a worrier, but tends to be rather passive. He is treated haughtily by Lady Bracknell and teased constantly by Algernon. Gwendolen takes the initiative in their courtship, even directing the way he should propose. In Act III, he takes a more active role; he enjoys being able to blackmail Lady Bracknell, and we enjoy watching him stand up to her.

Gwendolen

The more sophisticated of the two young ladies, Gwendolen has been trained to follow the dictates of fashion. She is the essence of artificially. She takes tea without sugar and bread and butter instead of cake because it is fashionable to do so. She uses a lorgnette (a type of spectacles) because her mother has taught her to be nearsighted.

It is interesting to note Gwendolen's relations with her mother, who orders her about constantly. There is nothing of rebellious youth about her. She does not object to her treatment; she simply says, "Yes, mamma," and then does as she pleases. In this, she is like Lord Goring in *An Ideal Husband*. He handles his overbearing father, Lord Caversham, in exactly the same way.

Gwendolen repeats most of the **cliches** of romantic heroines-but usually with a difference. She tells Jack she will always love him, even though her mother will not let her marry him. "But although she may prevent us from becoming man and wife, and I may marry someone else, and marry often, nothing that she can possibly do can alter my eternal devotion to you." Jack has no complaints over this odd expression of everlasting loyalty. He only says: "Dear Gwendolen."

In Act III, when Jack goes to get the handbag and show it to Miss Prism, he says: "Gwendolen, wait here for me." She answers: "If you are not too long, I will wait here for you all my life." In short, Gwendolen is a perfect romantic heroine, except that she does not care for personal inconvenience.

Algernon

He is a young man full of adventurous high spirits. Being in debt does not worry him; he tears up his bills quite cheerfully in Act I. Even the temporary anger of Cecily does not depress him. The fact that he pretends to be Ernest and invades Jack's house to meet Cecily shows how enterprising he is, and how fond of escapades.

Algernon has a marvelous appetite. He eats up his aunt's cucumber sandwiches in Act I and devours all Jack's muffins in Act II. Even when he falls in love with Cecily, he does not forget his stomach. He tells her that the first necessity for reformation of character is a good meal. His appetite emphasizes his youth and vitality.

Cecily

Though Cecily is young and naive, she exhibits a strong personality. With innocent charm, she causes Algernon to fall in love with her and propose to her, something she has had in mind for some time, since she has been engaged to him in her imagination for three months. She has even written a great number of letters to herself on his behalf!

This simple girl is able to take the honors in a verbal combat with Gwendolen, who is older and more experienced. This is another measure of her capabilities.

Cecily is gay, pert, and coy. She thus shows some relation to Mabel Chiltern in *An Ideal Husband*. But Mabel is rather difficult for a modern reader to enjoy. We must take her charm on trust, figuring that tastes change with time. Cecily, though, is authentically charming. When played by a skillful actress, she is entirely delightful.

Lady Bracknell

She is the final development of a long line of society matrons portrayed in Wilde's plays. She is certainly the most impressive of all. As Jack sadly describe her, she is a monster who is not a myth. Her will is of iron; so is her assurance. She never doubts her own ideas or standards. She runs the lives of her family as a matter of course. She is relentlessly logical, though her logic is of a kind only found in Wilde's plays. Speaking of her nephew Algernon as an eligible young man, she says: "He has nothing, but he looks everything. What more can one desire?"

Lady Bracknell is a capable trader in that marketplace where marriages are arranged among the upper classes. Her business-like instincts contrast amusingly with her social elegance.

Miss Prism

Miss Prism is the author of a very sentimental three-volume novel (this was the usual length of popular Victorian fiction), but her own attitudes are realistic. She keeps fact and fiction strictly separated. She is thoroughly unsentimental about the mythical Ernest. Upon hearing of his death, she comments that it will be a good lesson for him. She expresses honest dismay when it turns out that he is not dead after all.

Miss Prism is amusing in her awkward pursuit of Dr. Chasuble, a stubborn bachelor, in which she is successful at the end of the play.

We must conscientiously note also her mixing up a baby and a manuscript, a piece of absent-mindedness of classic proportions. However, Miss Prism shows no actual absent-mindedness during the play.

Dr. Chasuble

This conscientious elderly clergyman is the object of Miss Prism's respectable affection. He expresses suitable sentiments for each occasion during the play. We get the impression that he is not exactly a fascinating preacher. He plans to preach a sermon commemorating Ernest's death. It is a sermon he has used innumerable times. He adjusts it each time for the specific occasion, happy or sad. Everyone sighs when he mentions it. They have obviously sat through it many times; they do not look forward to hearing it once more.

Lord Bracknell

Lord Bracknell, father of Gwendolen and husband of Lady Bracknell, makes no appearance in the play. But from the references of his wife and daughter, a portrait emerges. Lady Bracknell does not tell him where Gwendolen has gone when she flees to visit Jack. She lets him think that Gwendolen is at a particular long university extension lecture. Earlier, she tells Gwendolen that her father will let her know when she is engaged, if his health permits. Gwendolen remarks that nobody has ever heard of her father; his proper place is in the home.

Perhaps the most vivid little picture is created by Lady Bracknell in Act I. She says that if Algernon does not come to dinner, it will spoil the symmetry of the dinner table. In that case, Lord Bracknell will have to dine alone upstairs. Luckily, he is used to it.

The absent Lord Bracknell is sketched as a feeble, ineffectual man, managed by his wife and ignored by his daughter. Though he is the host, he has to eat upstairs by himself during dinner parties, if his wife finds this convenient.

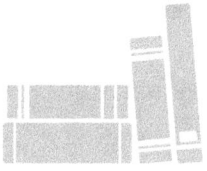

OSCAR WILDE

CRITICAL COMMENTARY

....

As we try to come to an understanding of Oscar Wilde's place in English literature, we must begin with the realization that he is not what we call a major writer. This is stated or assumed by most critics. By a major writer we mean one who has produced a substantial body of work, which is of uncommon quality, revealing exceptional gifts of thought, observation, and expression. Among British dramatic writers, of course Shakespeare stands in a class by himself. Nobody else is comparable to him. But Christopher Marlowe, William Congreve, Richard Brinsley Sheridan, George Bernard Shaw, and Sean O'Casey perhaps belong in the first rank of dramatic writers if we eliminate Shakespeare from consideration. Oscar Wilde does not have such an exalted place.

Yet, if Wilde is not the very greatest of writers, he is still an uncommonly interesting one. His biography alone has an enduring fascination. His extravagant behavior and quotable wit are the stuff that anecdotes are made of. Some of Wilde's work may fade into oblivion, but the stories about him have a quality of lasting vitality. Many a person who has never read a word of his writing knows about the man who wore a huge sunflower in his lapel, who once said he had stayed up all night with a sick primrose, who told a customs officer that he had nothing to declare except his genius.

Wilde's life also has a deeper significance. His story illustrates perfectly some of the most important characteristics of Victorian society. Wilde's family was colorful and talented, but it was not a part of the high nobility. However, in the years when Wilde flourished, he associated mainly with aristocratic Englishmen. These were leisured people with inherited wealth, cultivated tastes, and beautiful homes. In the select and severely limited society of these aristocratic families Wilde visited, drank tea, dined, danced, and above all talked. The lords and ladies were delighted to have him. They had enough education and taste to appreciate him. The fine old houses in London, the great houses in the country, all were open to him.

We must realize that this was the only society that had a place for a man like Wilde. While it is true that Wilde had little respect for the nouveau riche capitalists, these wealthy newcomers had little interest in him either. Wit, gaiety, and the appreciation of beauty had no place in the lives of mine and factory owners who were enjoying wealth for the first time. As a group, they were smug and materialistic. They spent their wealth on things that could make them comfortable and on things that would show they were rich, but they were not patrons of the arts. They did not yet understand that way of spending money. The appreciation of the arts as a part of an attitude toward life - this was still the province of the old aristocrats.

We may say, therefore, that if Wilde was a snob - and he was - he had little choice in the matter.

There is an enlightened discussion of Victorian snobbery and Victorian capitalists in Parrott and Martin's *A Companion to*

Victorian Literature. This modern American work (1955) is in refreshing contrast to some of the older British critics; many of them are convinced themselves that a "good family" is the most valuable thing a man can have. Inherently snobbish themselves, they can only defend Wilde's snobbishness passionately rather than examine it objectively.

Wilde began as a novelty in Victorian high society. He ended almost as a god. His words were sought and treasured. His witticisms were published. Even an insult from him was enough to give distinction to the one who received it. The delight which he inspired seemed boundless. In 1895, his fatal year, a brilliant society audience laughed at and cheered *The Importance of Being Earnest.* Never had an opening night been more wildly successful.

Within that same year Wilde was ruined. The very people who had cheered him most loudly turned on him most viciously. Little help or sympathy was given by his former friends. With horrible relish, they enjoyed each detail of his disastrous libel suit and his subsequent trial. They took pleasure in his humiliation and outdid each other in inventing ways to increase his misery-all in the name of righteousness.

The analysis of this behavior is what interests us, rather than Wilde's own sordid, commonplace history. What made a whole society act with such ferocity? In part it can no doubt be explained as the cruel pleasure people sometimes take in seeing anyone who is high and admired brought low. But more important was the nature of Victorian society, with its worship of respectability - not virtue, but a systematic concealment of weakness. For the Victorians, hypocrisy was an accepted morality. Therefore, when a hidden evil became known, it was natural for them to denounce it vigorously, to make up for the fact that many of them had their discreditable secrets too. People who have guilty secrets are extra loud in denouncing one among them who has been unlucky enough to get caught. This is well known to students of psychology. Thus Wilde was a sort of human sacrifice for the Victorians. By destroying him they celebrated the fact that they themselves were still safe.

The impact of Wilde's disaster on Victorian mores is carefully discussed in Hesketh Pearson's biography, *Oscar Wilde: His Life and Wit*. Frances Winwar fills in the background details of Victorian society in *Oscar Wilde and the Yellow Nineties*. We should also note in passing Frank Harris' biography of Wilde. Harris was an interesting writer who was a friend of many famous men, but he was naturally incapable of telling the truth. All his books are untrustworthy, none more so than his work on Wilde.

Wilde wrote extensively, but he did it mainly to make money. His poetry is verbose. It is a mixture of styles which he copied from many of his favorite poets, especially Swinburne and Byron. Only "The **Ballad** of Reading Gaol" (1898), that painful product of his imprisonment, has lasting value.

Among his prose writings, the fairy tales are lovely, with a jewelled artificiality that Wilde handled with much success.

The Picture of Dorian Gray, Wilde's only novel, is interesting because it shows clearly how much his work was modeled on French influences. A thorough understanding of French literature is valuable in the study of English writing in the eighteen nineties. We may say that without the poet Baudelaire and the novelists Flaubert and Zola, Dorian Gray could not exist. The best explanation of these French influences is to be found in Osbert Burdett's *The Beardsley Period*.

As a dramatist, Wilde accepted uncritically the popular practices of his day. *Lady Windermere's Fan, A Woman of No Importance,* and *An Ideal Husband* are full of the apparatus so dear to hack writers-family secrets, compromising letters, dilemmas, intrigues, and coincidences. All this material was used abundantly by Scribe, Sardou, and quantities of second-rate English writers now forgotten. Wilde adopted it uncritically. He was apparently not offended by its unreality.

Wilde was able to use this commonplace material efficiently. It was as though writing a play was a kind of game and the use of the letters and the secrets and all the rest was simply part of the rules.

In the above-mentioned plays we also observe some effort to introduce a serious problem, as if Wilde was conscious that a complicated plot was not enough of an excuse for a play's existence. But Wilde was not successful as a writer of problem plays. He did not have a probing, analytical intellect. His "problems" were familiar ones, to which the answers were a foregone conclusion. (Can a good woman who once made a misstep ever find forgiveness and happiness? Answer: Yes.)

Osbert Burdett, in *The Beardsley Period,* discusses Wilde's use of conventional formulae in writing his plays. He also shows awareness of Wilde's intellectual limitations.

A richly informative book on the drama of Wilde's time is Maurice Valency's *The Flower and the Castle.* The book is not about Wilde, but about the new drama of Ibsen and Strindberg and the changes it wrought in the theatre. The theatre of Scribe and Sardou is described, so that the effect of the daring Scandinavian geniuses is clearly understood in context.

For the student who desires to understand more about the drama of the late nineteenth century and Wilde's place in it, the study of a few plays by Ibsen, Strindberg and Shaw is recommended. For instance, consider Henrik Ibsen's play *Ghosts*. In this play Ibsen examines the problem of a woman who finds herself married to a dissolute man. She is unable to make him happy, and his bad qualities become worse as a result. He is lazy, drunken, and immoral. She is unspeakably miserable.

Ibsen feels that such a marriage should be broken up. He demonstrates that the child of such a marriage is bound to have a disastrous life. He suggests that the wife should have had the courage to elope with another man, whom she loved.

To read this play with its angry, cranky, individualistic viewpoint, is to gain insight into what the drama is capable of. It can be controversial, profound, stimulating, even infuriating. One does not have to agree with Ibsen to see that he has given the drama a new dimension. It becomes a forum for human insights, experiences, and doubts.

It is suggested that the student become acquainted with Ibsen's *Ghosts*, *A Doll's House*, and *An Enemy of the People*, Strindberg's *Miss Julie*, and Bernard Shaw's *Mrs. Warren's Profession*, *Man and Superman*, and *Major Barbara*. This will give balance and substance to his reading.

Most critics have noted that in Wilde's earlier plays (the ones we have been discussing), the action occasionally stops to permit the insertion of amusing minor characters and witty dialogue. We do not know exactly how Wilde got the inspiration to use only amusing characters and witty dialogue, and to turn the conventional plot into a **burlesque** of itself. The result was *The Importance of Being Earnest*. No adequate study has ever been made of how the **themes** and characters used by Wilde in the earlier plays reappear in *The Importance of Being Earnest*. Some suggestions are to be found in this book, in the chapters on the individual plays. The critics usually content themselves with appreciation of the play's lightness and wit. Allardyce Nicoll, in his valuable book, *World Drama*, remarks that Wilde's wit shatters the conventions of society. He also points out that Wilde's fondness for paradox shows his relation to another superlative Victorian humorist, William S. Gilbert, librettist for the Gilbert and Sullivan operettas. Gilbert too portrays a topsy-turvy world.

Most critics note the frivolous portrait of society we find in *The Importance of Being Earnest*. Maurice Valency points out that the portrait of society found in all the plays bears little relation to real life. He also observes that Wilde's frivolity is so determined that it suggests a kind of despair.

Indeed, Wilde's work does suggest a man making a perpetual effort to escape from something he does not want to look at. He is a rebel against Victorian life, every bit as much as William Morris or John Ruskin (see Introduction), though his rebellion is largely unconscious.

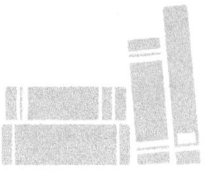

OSCAR WILDE

ESSAY QUESTIONS AND ANSWERS

Question: Describe the aesthetic movement of Oscar Wilde's time. What causes did it spring from? Are there any traces of it in Oscar Wilde's plays?

Answer: The aesthetic movement was probably a response to some of the ugly or depressing aspects of life in nineteenth-century England. These factors made it very difficult for some Englishmen to live contentedly in their environment.

One such factor was the Industrial Revolution, which transferred manufacturing from the home to the mass-production factory. This process began in eighteenth-century England but was accelerated in the nineteenth century. Before the Industrial Revolution there were very few sizable cities. After it, the major part of the population was to be found in the cities. The factories were built in towns near seaports, where raw materials such as coal, iron and wool could reach them easily, and from which the manufactured products could be shipped conveniently. To these towns the workers flocked. There was no effort to plan the growth of the towns. The result was a sprawling accumulation of slums, where housing had been thrown up in the cheapest possible way to accommodate the hordes of workers. In these slums, crowds of people lived amid dirt, poor sanitation, and, inevitably, disease. The cities, particularly those of the industrial north, were blots upon the landscape of England.

The products of the factories also represented a change. Large numbers of objects were produced with the help of machines. But the craftsman's pride which animated the man or woman who made something from beginning to end with his own hands was gone. Cheap, ugly, poorly made things replaced the solid, carefully made products of the older system.

Science, too, changed the world. A long series of scientific thinkers, including Charles Darwin, produced the theory of the evolutionary development of living species. This created a picture in which Nature used death and violence as the instruments by which life was shaped and developed. A universe which worked on the principle of "The Survival of the Fittest" was a depressing place, compared to one in which a benevolent creator marked each sparrow's fall.

Many decent, sensitive people therefore found Victorian England a depressing place. Their reactions were of various kinds. Some protested against social and economic conditions. John Ruskin pointed out the relation between degrading working conditions and ugly, poorly made products. Elizabeth Barrett Browning portrayed the horrors of child labor in her poetry. William Morris turned back to hand crafts in manufacturing, together with careful attention to working conditions.

But there were some who did not meet the evils of Victorian life head-on, as these did. (These were looked upon as dangerous radicals in their own time.) Some people took the route of escape. Ignoring rather than fighting the spiritual and physical pain which was always near, they turned to a contemplation of beauty. To respond to beauty completely became the highest good. Moral considerations were definitely secondary. The Pre-Raphaelites turned back to the art and poetry of the Middle Ages. Walter Pater turned imaginatively to the graceful aristocratic existence of ancient Rome. From this he formed the theory that the greatest good life has to offer is the use of the physical sensibilities. Each moment should hold its full quota of rich sensation.

To make sensation the supreme good, more urgent than ethical considerations, is a dangerous doctrine. Pater himself was a mild, conservative man in real life, but he influenced many Oxford students with his amoral doctrine. One of these was Oscar Wilde.

Wilde became convinced that the full appreciation of beauty is the main business of existence. In his twenties, he devoted much energy to the creation of beautiful surroundings, beautiful clothing, and other things which made up a life of rich sensation. Later on, when he turned his energies largely to writing, he would occasionally create characters who were spokesmen for these ideas. Interestingly, these characters were almost always unsympathetic.

The most conspicuous example of such a character in Wilde's plays is Lord Illingworth in *A Woman of No Importance*. When social reform is mentioned, he indicates that the subject is morbid. Human beings should not think about ugliness; they should focus only on joy and beauty. Later in the play, he states, only half-jokingly that the proper tying of a necktie is one of the most important concerns of life. Lord Illingworth is, however, one of the most completely unsympathetic characters in Wilde's plays. It would seem from this that Wilde must have recognized that a purely aesthetic philosophy would probably make a person morally blind.

Question: Identify the literary sources of Oscar Wilde's dramatic writing.

Answer: Oscar Wilde turned to writing for the London theatre in the 1890s, not because of any powerful creative motivation, but because he hoped that he would be able to make a lot of money without a lot of effort by doing so. Thus, he did not have any new theories of dramatic art that he wanted to try out. He was not interested in introducing innovations in form, language or characterization. It was his intention to write popular plays. He therefore took as his model those plays which seemed to have wide audience appeal.

The most popular kind of play at the time was that which was derived from the French drama., These plays were notable mainly for their competent construction. Complex situations were clearly presented, one dramatic crisis followed another, the sympathetic and unsympathetic characters alternately gained the advantage, and at last all the complications were cleared up so that those who deserved to might live happily ever after. All other virtues were subordinated to movement and excitement. In plays like this, there was little room for subtlety or for rich characterization. The characters had to be drawn clearly and superficially, so that they could be easily understood.

This type of play was first popularized by Eugene Scribe. This writer developed play construction into almost an exact science. He even had a schedule or diagram showing which character should confront which at each point in the play. Scribe became the supervisor of a sort of mass production setup which produced hundreds of these plays-plays which appeared under Scribe's name.

It was a firm belief of Scribe that the purpose of the theatre was solely entertainment. No ideas or arguments on serious subjects should spoil the theatre's function as an escape from life's problems.

A second nineteenth-century French playwright who wrote in this mode was Victorien Sardou. Sardou belonged to a later generation, and his plays tended to be melodramas while Scribe's were comedies. But Sardou too concentrated on ingenious construction and effective scenes. Some of his plays were written for Sarah Bernhardt, the famous actress.

Plays of the kind developed by Scribe and Sardou held the popular stage in the 1890s. It is true that there was beginning to be an uneasy feeling in some quarters: was something missing from these plays? The great Scandinavians, Ibsen and Strindberg, had already demonstrated how deeply the drama could probe into human problems. In England, George Bernard Shaw, with a superb blend of gaiety and intellect, was starting on his great dramatic career.

Some English dramatists were trying to enjoy the advantages of both methods, the popular and the intellectual. They wrote plays in the old tradition but inserted intellectual discussions into them (or at least they were meant to be intellectual discussions.) The subject most often discussed was: Can a woman who has been guilty of unconventional behavior ever return to respectable society? This discussion usually lacked intellectual power. Often, it was filled with sentimental cliches. But it gave the audience the impression that they were watching something profound. Arthur Wing Pinero and Henry Arthur Jones were the best known playwrights of this type. Oscar Wilde's plays also reflect this style.

To summarize, Wilde's plays were conservative, following the methods of Scribe and Sardou. However, he sometimes tried to give the impression of being in the new intellectual group of writers by inserting some reference to social or human problems. These efforts are not very successful. The play which is most pretentious, *A Woman of No Importance*, is Wilde's worst play.

Question: Describe three types of wit used by Wilde in his plays.

Answers: Oscar Wilde had a lifelong reputation as an amusing conversationalist. Those who spent time with him always remembered the charm and gaiety of his talk. His wit consisted mostly of wild nonsense, paradox, and inverted logic. It was only natural for Wilde to use these same elements in his plays when he wanted comic material. Most people who knew Wilde personally have remarked that the comic material in his plays was simply his wonderful talk, written down.

Paradox is perhaps most characteristic of Wilde's wit. It is a statement which appears contradictory and is often the opposite of conventionally-held views. Such is Algernon's remark that divorces are made in Heaven, or Lady Bracknell's description of Lady Harbury, changed completely by her husband's death: "I never saw a woman so altered; she looks quite twenty years younger." Sometimes we are merely amused by the absurdity of the upside-down statement. In other cases it develops an unexpected quality of cynical observation, as in the second sample above.

Then there is sheer nonsense, which we enjoy for its extravagant absurdity, such as Lane's report that no cucumbers were available in the market, not even for ready money. Another delightful example occurs in *Lady Windermere's Fan*. Lady Agatha has been carefully directed by her mother, the Duchess of Berwick, until an eligible young man seems just about to propose to her. Lady Agatha never says anything during the course of the play except, "Yes, Mamma." As the young man takes Agatha to dance, her mother says: "Mind you take great care of my little chatterbox, Mr. Hopper." This inaccurate description of one of the least talkative girls imaginable is inspired nonsense.

The third variety of wit, the use of logic which sounds reasonable, but is preposterous, is found in all four of the plays. A good example occurs when Algernon asks Jack why Jack's aunt signs herself, "Your little Cecily." Jack replies: "Some aunts are tall, some aunts are not tall. That is a matter that surely an aunt may be allowed to decide for herself."

However, faulty logic is most often to be found among the society matrons who appear in each one of the plays. The Duchess of Berwick remarks that Australia has an odd shape on the map, but after all it is a young country. Lady Markby (*An Ideal Husband*) states that intellectual pressure makes the nose large and thus can make a young girl unmarriageable.

Lady Bracknell gives the most impressive display of this trait. Her logic is so consistently peculiar that she almost manages to reorganize our concepts of cause and effect. Jack confesses that he has lost both his parents. Lady Bracknell replies: "Both? . . . That seems like carelessness." It seems as though anybody might lose one parent, but if a person loses both, it must be his own fault.

To summarize: Paradox, nonsense, and faulty logic are three important elements of the wit we find in Oscar Wilde's plays. All four plays contain some of each, but *The Importance of Being Earnest* offers the richest examples.

Question: What moral principles are the basis of Wilde's plays?

Answer: Wilde did not have much talent for strictly intellectual analysis. Besides this, he was inclined by nature to absorb ideas from his environment. It is not surprising, therefore, to observe that there are no startling moral ideas in Wilde's plays. When he wanted to insert some ethical problem in a play and so produce an impression of profundity, he chose the question of sexual standards. This was an easy choice, since it commanded immediate interest. Thus, in *Lady Windermere's Fan*, Wilde demonstrates that the line separating the "good" woman from the "bad" woman is very thin. In *A Woman of No Importance*, Wilde shows how a woman may suffer all her life through while a man pays no penalty, even though they have been parties to the same sin. He also shows that the woman deserves forgiveness after she has spent many years expiating her sin. *An Ideal Husband* shows that it is unwise for a woman to judge her husband or try to control his destiny.

It can be seen that none of these ideas is even faintly revolutionary, although Wilde presents them with an air of significant discovery. In fact, they are based on the most conventional of Victorian notions. These assumptions are: that sexual relations outside marriage constitute the worst possible sin a human being can be guilty of; that once woman transgresses in this way she becomes forever a social outcast; that in the application of these rules, it is occasionally wise to consider the circumstances and grant forgiveness-but only after a long period of expiation has cleansed the sinner. Also, the wife is the subservient partner in marriage. Her function is to comfort her husband, never to criticize him.

To summarize, the moral ideas expressed in Wilde's plays are typical of his time. They are not startling nor revolutionary.

Question: What is Wilde's relation to Ibsen, Strindberg, and Shaw, the revolutionary dramatists of his time?

Answer: Oscar Wilde wrote for the theatre at a time when a most important change was taking place in the drama. During most of the nineteenth century, good English writers did not write plays. They devoted themselves to other kinds of literature, such as poetry and the novel. On rare occasions, a writer of genius tried to write plays but failed to write anything that could hold the interest of an audience. Shelley and Browning are two writers who made such attempts.

On the stage, performances of Shakespeare were popular. However, Shakespeare's plays were so cut up, changed around, and otherwise "improved" that they were sometimes hard to recognize. There were modern plays too. These were farces and melodramas, often copied from French models, and historical dramas full of crowds and spectacles.

In short, there was almost nothing on the English stage to interest an intelligent person. The commonplace fare of the theatre did not attract thoughtful people.

This was changed by the writings of the Norwegian dramatist Henrik Ibsen, who used plays as vehicles for his ideas. He showed that a play could probe deep into human problems and come up with suggested solutions which might cause shock or anger in an audience, but not boredom or indifference. His investigation of the man-woman relationship was especially profound.

Ibsen was a Norwegian, but eventually his plays were translated and performed on the English stage. They made a deep impression on a dramatic critic named George Bernard Shaw. When Shaw tried his playwriting, Ibsen was his inspiration. Shaw's first plays were, like Ibsen's unsparing original examinations of important problems. For example, *Widowers' Houses* is a play about the profits of slum landlords. It makes the uncomfortable point that all people live off such profits to some extent, even if they do not realize it, for nobody knows where the money he lives on originally comes from.

What was Wilde's response to these new voices heard in the drama? Almost none. Wilde's are conventional melodramas of the old-fashioned kind, full of intrigue and complications. Wilde was not basically given to criticism, either of men or of social institutions; he lacked an analytical intellect.

However, Wilde seemed to have some feeling that a premise or an idea was a requirement for a successful modern play. So he did what other playwrights were doing; he tried to give the impression of taking up a problem in each play, without really changing the old-fashioned nature of the play or saying anything that would startle anybody. For example, in Lady Windermere's Fan, he says that there can be a lot of good in a "bad" woman, as well as potentialities for sin in a "good" woman.

In *The Importance of Being Earnest*, Wilde gave up any pretense of writing a "modern" play. He simply wrote an old-fashioned play that made fun of itself. The path of true love does not run smooth mainly because the two heroines are determined to marry men named Ernest. What could better suggest the artificial character of most barriers to happy endings in the average melodrama?

Question: Discuss the **satire** in Wilde's plays.

Answer: As has been said, Oscar Wilde did not possess a critical temperament. To find out and then explain what was wrong with any person or social institution was never his main interest. So he is not primarily a satirist.

However, **satire** is found in Wilde's plays. There is an occasional touch of it in the three earlier plays. It is more extensive in *The Importance of Being Earnest*. However, the **satire** is of a light glancing kind. It is neither fierce nor extensive. It usually involves a good-natured gibe at social affectation or absurdity.

The portrait of Gwendolen Fairfax is a good example of Wilde's satire. Gwendolen gives the impression of having intelligence and a strong personality. Yet she is regulated in the smallest detail by what is proper or fashionable. She gazes at Cecily through a lorgnette because her mother has taught her to be nearsighted. She takes tea without sugar and bread and butter rather than cake, not because of any personal preference, but because they are fashionable refreshments. When Cecily gives her unfashionable refreshments she is moved to fury. The methods by which marriages were arranged between eligible young men and available young women, usually by the mothers of the latter, is also an object of Wilde's **satire**. Lady Bracknell has a list of eligibles which she shares with a duchess. "We work together," she says. In the matter of marriage, she is entirely the businesswoman. She takes out a pad and a pencil to note down Jack's replies to her questions. Lady Bracknell is foreshadowed in Wilde's portrait of the Duchess of Berwick in *Lady Windermere's*

Fan, who marries off her obedient daughter Agatha in a well-planned, efficient manner. As she checks over Agatha's dance program and tells her to go out on the terrace with Mr. Hopper, she is like a careful general planning a campaign. She may be fuzzy-headed about other things, such as whether kangaroos get around by crawling or flying, but she thinks quite clearly when she plans her daughter's engagement.

Oscar Wilde's plays contain literary **satire** as well as social satire. A fine example of this is Miss Prism's ancient error, described in *The Importance of Being Earnest*. When she was a nursemaid employed by the Moncrieff family, Miss Prism one day intended to put the baby in its carriage. She also meant to put the manuscript of a huge novel she had written into a handbag or valise. Instead, she put the manuscript into the carriage and the baby into the handbag, which she subsequently checked in the cloakroom of Victoria Station.

This madly improbable series of happenings is a **satire** on many plays and operas whose plots depended on mistakes made by nursemaids and identities revealed after many years of mystery. Giuseppe Verdi's opera *Il Trovatore* is one example of a work with a plot of this kind; it is meant to be taken quite seriously.

To summarize, we may say that although we do not think of Wilde primarily as a satirist, his plays do have satirical elements; the **satire** is light and good-natured. It deals with the foibles of society and the **conventions** of literature.

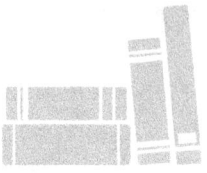

OSCAR WILDE

BIBLIOGRAPHY

Works Of Oscar Wilde

The plays of Oscar Wilde are available in many convenient editions. One of the easiest to obtain is the Modern Library edition, which contains the four plays discussed in this book as well as Salome.

A one-volume edition of Wilde's works was published in England by Spring Books in 1963. Though its small print prevents it from being an ideal reading edition, it yet makes available two early plays of Wilde which are otherwise difficult to obtain. These are *Vera, or the Nihilists*, and *The Duchess of Padua*, a verse play. These have little literary value, but they are of interest for the person who studies Wilde's development as a dramatist.

Biographies Of Oscar Wilde

Hyde, H. Montgomery, *Oscar Wilde: the Aftermath*. New York: 1963. An account of Wilde's years in prison, this book gives a horrifying picture of English prison conditions at the time. The author is a British lawyer and criminologist.

Pearson, Hesketh, *Oscar Wilde: His Life and Wit.* New York: 1946. A readable general biography of Wilde, which emphasizes anecdotal material.

Winwar, Frances, *Oscar Wilde and the Yellow Nineties.* New York: 1940. This book discusses the eccentric and decadent elements in Wilde's life which led him to disaster. It covers the material on Wilde's relationship to the Gilbert and Sullivan operetta *Patience* thoroughly.

Biographies Of Oscar Wilde's Family

Byrne, Patrick, *The Wildes of Merriam Square.* London and New York: 1953. An investigation of Oscar Wilde's immediate family, especially his gifted but dissipated father. His mother's portrait it also well drawn.

Wyndham, Horace, *Speranza.* New York: 1951. A biography of Oscar Wilde's mother. (Speranza was the pen-name she used when she wrote passionate essays in favor of Irish Nationalism.)

Books About The Eighteen-Nineties

Burdett, Osbert, *The Beardsley Period.* London: 1925. This study of the aesthetic movement of the nineties emphasizes the contribution of Aubrey Beardsley, a gifted illustrator whose somewhat decadent style decorated many books of the period, including Wilde's Salome.

Jackson, Holbrook, *The Eighteen Nineties.* New York: 1927. A minutely detailed history of the period. It is a most valuable reference work, but it is not designed to be read through from beginning to end.

BRIGHT NOTES STUDY GUIDE

Studies Of The Drama

Cunliffe, J. W., *Modern English Playwrights.* New York: 1927. A useful study of the English drama in Wilde's time and after. The contributions of individual playwrights are summarized.

Lewisohn, Ludwig, *The Modern Drama.* New York, 1915. An important discussion of the main developments of modern drama.

Nicoll, Allardyce, *World Drama.* New York: 1927. Revised. An encyclopedic book on all phases of the drama. It covers a great deal and therefore cannot go into detail.

Sawyer, N. W., *The Comedy of Manners from Sheridan to Maugham.* Philadelphia: 1931. This book provides a discussion of the development of polite comedy. It gives much information about other writers whose purposes were similar to Wilde's.

Valency, Maurice J., *The Flower and the Castle.* New York: 1963. The relationship between the drama of Scribe and Sardou, and that of Ibsen and Strindberg is fully discussed. A valuable book for anyone interested in the theatre.

Books About Victorian Literature

Baker, Joseph E. (editor), *The Reinterpretation of Victorian Literature.* Princeton, 1950. See especially Emery Neff's essay, "Social Background and Social Thought."

Buckley, Jerome H., *The Victorian Temper.* Cambridge: 1951. (Vintage paperback.)

Cooke, John D. and Lionel Stevenson, *English Literature of the Victorian Period.* New York: 1949. A handbook containing much useful information in a short space.

Parrott, Thomas Marc, and Robert Bernard Martin, *A Companion to Victorian Literature.* New York: 1955. Another good handbook.

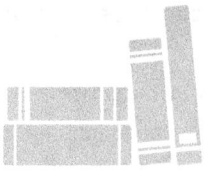

SUGGESTIONS FOR FURTHER READING

The reading of plays by Ibsen, Strindberg and Shaw as a contrast to Wilde's work has been suggested. The plays of Congreve (especially *Love for Love* and *The Way of the World*), the English dramatist most similar to Wilde in style and purpose, also make interesting reading.

For those students who are interested in nineteenth-century English society and its effect on literature, there are many avenues to explore. The English novel is a treasure-trove. The novels of Charles Dickens show many abuses of the time such as child labor and wretched schools. Thomas Hardy's novels are a conservative protest against the way the village life of England was disappearing; Samuel Butler's *The Way of All Flesh* demonstrates the way the closely knit family with the all-powerful father at its head was beginning to disintegrate.

Biographies of major Victorian figures are informative. Lytton Strachey's biography of Queen Victoria is unfriendly but lively. Margaret R. Grennan's *William Morris: Medievalist and Revolutionary* gives a portrait of the remarkable man who tried to undo the Industrial Revolution single-handed. These are only two of many available works.

www.ingramcontent.com/pod-product-compliance
Lightning Source LLC
LaVergne TN
LVHW011711060526
838200LV00051B/2859